Analysis, Design, and Implementation of Data Dictionaries

Analysis, Design, and Implementation of Data Dictionaries

Ken S. Brathwaite

McGraw-Hill Book Company

New York   St. Louis   San Francisco   Auckland
Bogotá   Hamburg   London   Madrid   Mexico
Milan   Montreal   New Delhi   Panama
Paris   São Paulo   Singapore
Sydney   Tokyo   Toronto

Library of Congress Cataloging-in-Publication Data

Brathwaite, Ken S.
  Analysis, design, and implementation of data dictionaries / Ken S.
  Brathwaite.

      p.   cm.
    Bibliography: p.
    Includes index.
    ISBN 0-07-007248-5 : $39.95
      1. Data base management.   2. Data dictionaries.   I. Title.
QA76.9.D3B688 1988
005.74'2—dc19   87-20983
                                                                     CIP

Copyright © 1988 by McGraw-Hill, Inc. All rights reserved. Printed in
the United States of America. Except as permitted under the United
States Copyright Act of 1976, no part of this publication may be
reproduced or distributed in any form or by any means, or stored in a
data base or retrieval system, without the prior written permission of the
publisher.

1234567890   DOC/DOC   893210987

ISBN 0-07-007248-5

                    Braithwaite, Ken S.
      QA
      76.9   Analysis, design,
      .D3   and implementation
      B688   of data dictionar-
      1988   ies

                        55,623

The editors for this book were Theron Shreve and Georgia
Kornbluth, the designer was Naomi Auerbach, and the production
supervisor was Dianne Walber. It was set in Century Schoolbook by
BYRD Press.

Printed and bound by R. R. Donnelley & Sons Company.

To Monique, Marguerite,
Michele, and Melanie.
I love you all.

CAMROSE LUTHERAN COLLEGE
LIBRARY

CONTENTS

To My Readers

The express purpose of this book is to discuss in a meaningful way the analysis, design, and implementation of data dictionaries.

The book starts off with a discussion of the environments in which data dictionaries are used. Some of these include environments in which data analysis is done in a methodical fashion and extensive use is made of the data dictionary to record the results of the analysis phase. Another is the information center, where users can obtain solutions for their problems. The data dictionary is a valuable tool in defining and describing the essential data elements that may be of interest to the user—hence the discussion of these environments.

The intent of this book is to enable readers to develop their own in-house data dictionaries to meet their own unique requirements. Readers will quickly determine that, in some chapters, more emphasis is placed on the discussion of background material than on the actual development of the data dictionary for the particular environment. The reasoning behind this approach is that if the reader understands the environment, then the development of the dictionary for that environment becomes a simple matter. Thus the chapters on the use of data dictionaries in online and distributed data-processing, office automation, and data-security environments place heavy emphasis on the understanding of these environments.

The design aspect of data dictionaries centers on the metadata (entries) and standards that must be incorporated into average data dictionaries. Several chapters, including Chapter 3, are devoted to these entries and standards. Readers may want to incorporate all these entries into their data dictionaries or may prefer to select those entries that best describe their data requirements.

A data dictionary can be implemented by creating a database from the entries described in this book, using any of the currently available utilities to load the database and a teleprocessing (TP) monitor to retrieve information from the data dictionary. Chapter 4 discusses a typical implementation of a data dictionary and gives an example of the entries retrieved from the dictionary.

The book ends with case histories of actual usage of data dictionaries in two corporations. The case histories are unedited and were obtained by sending surveys to various companies.

PREFACE

The work reported in this book was developed from notes I used in teaching a course for graduate students at the University of Alberta and from research conducted at Alberta Government Telephones since 1981. The book is intended to serve as a practical guide for workers at all levels who are responsible for designing and implementing data dictionaries.

The main objective of this book is to provide material that is essential for the efficient design and implementation of data dictionary systems. The book provides workers with the tools necessary for either selecting data dictionary designs that will be adequate for their environments or developing their own in-house dictionary systems.

The content of the book has been considerably enhanced by my experience as a member of the American National Standards Institute (ANSI) X3H4 Committee, responsible for establishing standards for data dictionaries.

The report on the usage of data dictionaries in various companies reflects the results of surveys sent to the Fortune 500 companies in the United States and the Financial Post 500 companies in Canada. The surveys sought to determine the type of dictionary in use (whether a manufacturer's or one developed in-house) in each company, the history and usage of the dictionary, whether the dictionary was used in an active or a passive manner, the maintenance requirements of the dictionary, and the special reports produced by the dictionary.

Part I introduces the environments in which a dictionary may be used. Chapter 1 details those environments and covers such topics as (1) data analysis and functional analysis, (2) logical and physical design, (3) documentation, (4) data security and integrity, and (5) user and information center requirements.

Chapter 2 introduces the basic concepts of the data dictionary and covers the definition of a data dictionary, active versus passive data dictionaries, case histories of data dictionary uses, entries and contents of data dictionaries, and the concept of metadata.

Chapter 3 deals with the design of in-house dictionaries. It discusses the reasons for developing your own dictionary, the planning requirements for development of the dictionary, and an implementable structure for an in-house dictionary. Chapter 4 discusses a method of entering data into an in-house data dictionary.

Chapters 5 and 6 discuss the results of surveys conducted in two environments—distributed data processing and office automation—to determine how dictionaries were used in those environments. Chapter 7 deals with the security aspects of the data dictionary. It illustrates not only how to secure the contents of the data dictionary but how to use the data dictionary to achieve both data security and physical security.

Chapter 8 discusses the dictionary as a tool for automated physical database design. It shows how a dictionary can be used to store information about the attributes, entities, and logical schemas which are used to build the physical databases. The designer can use the known relationships among these entries to automatically group and produce the building blocks required for database design. Chapter 9 shows how standards are developed and used in a data dictionary environment.

Chapter 10 discusses performance indicators in data dictionaries. It shows ways in which users can collect and use statistics to determine how well a dictionary is performing in relation to the needs of the particular environment.

Part II presents case histories of dictionaries and how they are being used in various organizations.

ACKNOWLEDGMENTS

I am grateful for the comments and suggestions I received from Vic Howard, Stan Locke, and Francis Chin. The initial draft of this manuscript was ably typed by Jane Cuffy. Her efforts are appreciated.

Ken S. Brathwaite

Analysis, Design, and Implementation of Data Dictionaries

Part

1

Concepts of
Data Dictionaries

1

Introduction to Data Dictionaries and the Database Environment

Introduction

This chapter discusses what a data dictionary is and the various database environments in which it is used. The *data dictionary* can be defined as an organized reference to the data content of the organization. The content may be a program, a system, a database, or a collection of all the files and manual records maintained by the organization.

Over the past several years the data dictionary has been used as a tool by data administrators to document and maintain the names and definitions of the data items in the data base. However, with the increasing recognition of data as a corporate resource and the need to manage the resources more efficiently, data administrators are putting the data dictionary to several different uses.

The next several sections describe some of the uses of the data dictionary.

1.1 The Data Dictionary as a Glossary of Definitions

One use of the data dictionary is as a glossary of terms, whether about the entire organization or for entire systems. The glossary allows users to communicate with one another using common terms and definitions.

The data dictionary can also be used as a glossary of data items. In this case a few lines or paragraphs are dedicated to defining each data item used in the database environment.

1.2 The Data Dictionary as a Systems-Development and Systems-Maintenance Tool

The data dictionary can be very effective when used as a tool to support structured analysis and design. It can be used to document data items, data flow, and process definitions. As such, it is an efficient way of portraying systems-design details to the user.

The data dictionary can also be used to generate file, segment, and record definitions for a variety of programming languages. This use can centralize the control of program data definitions, in order to ensure consistency of data use and inhibit data redundancy.

Its ability to centralize the control of data use makes the data dictionary a very effective tool in change-control management. The data dictionary is the origin of all data definitions, and so any new data requirements must have the knowledge and approval of data administration.

Because the dictionary enforces consistency of data naming and format variation, it significantly reduces the cost of program maintenance.

1.3 The Data Dictionary as a Superior Documentation Medium

Documentation stored in a data dictionary is available to anyone who has access to a computer terminal. The automated search and cross-referencing tools of a data dictionary can span multiple programs, systems, databases, report definitions, form definitions, or any other entity type.

The data dictionary can be used to generate the source-program data definitions; the data portion of the program is actually derived from the documentation.

1.4 Contents of a Typical Data Dictionary

The contents of a typical data dictionary can be generally classified into three groups: data contents, processing contents, and environment contents.

Data contents describe or represent dictionary entries which are units of data—for example, attributes, entities, segments, and databases.

Processing contents describe or represent dictionary entries which are processes, systems, programs, and transactions.

Environment contents describe or represent dictionary entries which are associated with the physical environment—for example, security features, users, terminals, and audit techniques.

The next several sections will serve to introduce the environments in which data dictionaries are currently being used:

- Data analysis and functional analysis
- Logical and physical design
- Documentation
- Data security and integrity
- Management reports
- User and information center requirements
- Data administration and database administration
- Standards and naming conventions
- Change control
- Hardware and software performance statistics
- Consistency checks

In understanding the sections which follow and the environments in which the data dictionary flourishes, the following definitions will be useful:

1. *Entity.* A fundamental thing of interest to an organization. An entity may be a person, thing, concept, or event and may be real or abstract. "Entity" and "entity class" are used interchangeably in some of the literature, but some researchers define an *entity* as an occurrence of an entity class. For example, "employee" is an entity class, whereas "S. T. Locke," an occurrence of the entity class "employee," is an entity.

2. *Attribute.* A descriptive value or property associated with an individual entity. Attributes can be classified, by one or more rules,

Data Contents	Processing Contents	Environment Contents
Attribute	System	Security features
Relationship	Program	Users
Entity	Transaction	Audit techniques
Segment	Retrieval languages	Terminals
Database		Organization
Screen		
Report		
Logical schema		

Figure 1.1 Three groups of data dictionary contents

as describing an entity, uniquely identifying an entity, describing relationships between entities, and being used to derive attributes.

3. *Relationship.* An association between two or more entities. For example, "employed by" is a relationship between an employee and employer.

4. *Segment.* The smallest unit of information that a retrieval language, e.g., Data Language (DL/1), can handle when working with information in the database.

5. *Database.* A collection of files, records, groups, and elements stored according to the constraints of a particular database management system (DBMS).

6. *Database management system.* The software that allows one or more persons to use the data stored in a database, to modify it, or to do both.

1.5   Data Analysis and Functional Analysis

Data analysis is the process of determining the fundamental data resources of an organization. It deals with the collection of a description of the basic entities and the relationships among the entities.

The primary purpose of data analysis is to organize and document all relevant facts concerning the organization's data resource.

Data analysis has been used to

- Determine the fundamental data resources of an organization.
- Provide a disciplined approach to cataloguing the existing data in terms of the entities and relationships represented.
- Provide effective means of communicating with non-data-processing users, as it deals only with things that the users are familiar with and not with such objects as files and records.
- Analyze the inherent structure of that data independently of the details of the applications.
- Form a basis for data-control, security, and auditing systems.
- Organize all relevant facts concerning the organization's data.
- Produce a point of reference—the entity model—against which a logical database structure for each of the database management systems can be designed.
- Provide a sound basis for database design.

Data analysis is regarded as consisting of two dependent projects:

- Entity analysis, which provides a means of understanding and documenting a complex environment in terms of its entities and their attributes and relationships.

- Functional analysis, which is concerned with understanding and documenting the basic activities of the organization (Figure 1.2).

1.6 Functional Analysis

Functional analysis is concerned with an understanding and documentation of the basic business activities with which the organization is concerned. Functional analysis has the following objectives:

- To determine how entities are used so as to increase understanding of the entity model

- To provide a firm basis for transaction design

- To gather estimates of data usage for database design

Functional analysis may reveal attribute types of entities which had not been detected during entity analysis. Similarly, relationships between entities which had not been considered meaningful may be found to be required by certain functions.

The basic functions identified in functional analysis would be expected to be translated into transaction types in the data-processing system.

Estimates of data usage will provide a means for determining which access paths should be made most efficient.

Functional analysis can be divided into the following phases:

- Preliminary analysis

- Developing a framework

- Access-path analysis

In functional analysis the application area which is to be analyzed must be defined. The application area may coincide with the data area examined in the data analysis, or it may cross several data areas. Here *data area* may be defined as the data utilized in areas determined by the organizational structure, e.g., accounting, personnel, manufacturing, marketing, and purchasing.

In the process of developing a framework, the analyst identifies the events and functions. An *event* may be defined as a stimulus to the organization, and *functions* may be defined as tasks that must be carried out as a direct result of the event.

1.7   Example of Functional Analysis

One of the functions identified as being carried out in the order-processing area is order entry. An order is received from a delivery point. Selection of the depot that will make the delivery is made on the basis of whether the goods are bulk or packaged. The order is recorded and related to the delivery point and the depot. The goods specified in each order line are validated, and the stocks of the goods on hand are amended. Where stocks are insufficient to meet the quantities in one or more lines in the order, a back order is created. The order lines are recorded and linked to the goods and to the order or back order as appropriate.

The functional entity model resulting from the above description is shown in Figure 1.2. The rectangles represent entities, and the straight lines connecting the rectangles are the relationships of the entities. The diagram indicates that an order is sent to a delivery point, an order is made up of order lines, goods are taken from stock, and the stock is held in a depot.

1.8   The Entity Model

The major output of the data-analysis phase of database design is the entity model. The entity model is a diagrammatical representation of the relationships among the entities. The representation allows us to include only those entities that are required to solve the particular data-processing problem.

The entity model is essentially a real-world view of the data in terms of entities, attributes, and relationships. The entity model is used by the data-analysis team to

- Reduce redundancy in the relationship.
- Determine which entities are significant to the model and the requirement of the problem.

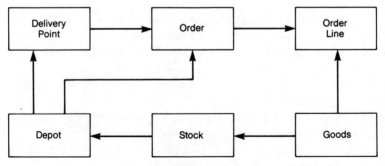

Figure 1.2 Functional entity model for order entry

1.9   Revisions of the Entity Model

Revisions of the entity model are done for the following reasons:

- To produce the optimum model
- To normalize the entities
- To synthesize the relationships

1.10   Approaches to Producing the Entity Model

The entity model can be produced using either a bottom-up or a top-down approach. The bottom-up approach produces a composite or global view of the organization's data based on the integration of several users' views of the immediate problems requirements, and not on the inherent structure of the data. The resulting model is limited to the immediate problem and cannot reflect the entire business activities of the organization.

The top-down approach produces a global, corporate, or organizational view of the data before the application views are identified. The entities and relationships which are of interest to the organization are identified from the business activities of the total organization and independently of any particular application.

The bottom-up approach is the one most often used in data analysis. This approach produces a model with more clearly defined boundaries than the top-down approach. The processing requirements can be used by the data-analysis team to determine precisely what entities are required and the composition of these entities. The clustering of attributes into their respective entities or the splitting of entities can be done with more precision. This approach makes it easier to determine whether an attribute is indeed an attribute of an existing entity or is itself an entity with relationships to other entities.

1.11   Selection and Identification of Entities

Data analysis permits the selection and identification of entities in the following three ways:

- By one or more attributes
- By the combination of a relationship with one or more attributes
- By two or more relationships

In the simplest case of entity identification, each occurrence of the attribute has a unique value which is used to identify the entity. Combinations of attributes may also be used, as when employees are identified by their names and the dates they joined the company.

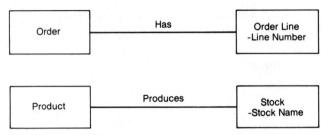

Figure 1.3 Entity identification by relationships

The members of the relationship are often uniquely identified within that relationship by the values of the attribute type, but for uniqueness within the system the owner of the relationship needs also to be known. In effect, it is the relationship occurrence, as identified by its owner, which is contributing to the unique identification of its members.

An example of entity identification by relationships and attributes is illustrated in Figure 1.3.

1.12   Example of an Entity Model

The following example will serve to illustrate the use of entity modeling in database design. The database application illustrated below is a general payroll application. The relevant department consists of a number of employees. The department wishes to process employees' paychecks and pensions. The pensions can be paid in a lump sum or in installments upon retirement, death, or resignation of an employee. In addition to the processing of paychecks and pensions, the department wishes to make inquiries about the projects a particular employee has worked on.

The entities and relationships from the above case study are shown in the entity model (Figure 1.4).

1.13   Discussion of the Entity Model

Let us examine three of the entities of the above model. Some typical attributes of those entities are shown below.

Entity	Typical attribute
Department	Department number, name, head, description
Employee	Employee number, social security number, name, address, status, supervisor, hourly rate
Pensions	Pensions identifier, type, description, amount

In the "department" and "employee" entities the attributes "head" and "supervisor" best describe another entity. We can now create a new entity, "manager," and replace the two attributes with pointers or relationships to the original entities. We can also add new attributes to the entity "manager."

Some typical attributes of "manager" are as follows:

Entity	Typical Attributes
Manager	Manager identifier, name, authority

The two relationships that we must now establish are *manager-department* and *manager-employee*.

In the "pension" entity the attribute "type" indicates that pensions can be paid upon retirement, death, or resignation of employees, in a lump sum, annually, or as deferred payments.

Because of the queries the users want to make, it may be desirable to split the "pensions" entity into one or more entities. For example, we may have one entity for natural retirements and another for all lump-sum payments. In this case the entities are application views of the "pensions" entity.

1.14   Further Revisions of the Entity Model

Revisions of the entity model may be necessary when new information about the entities and relationships is discovered. These revisions may involve splitting or merging the entities or determining when an

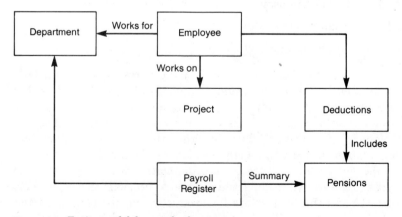

Figure 1.4 Entity model for paycheck processing

attribute of an entity is best treated as an entity in its own right, related to the first entity.

The following rules apply when making revisions to the entity model:

- Determine if the attribute itself has any other related attributes.
- Determine if the new entity is required to solve the data-processing problem.
- Determine if the attribute in fact identifies the second entity.
- Determine if the new entity is related to the original entity.
- Determine if the new entity is related to any other entities in the model.

1.15 Clustering of Entity Classes

Clustering of entity classes in database design may occur in the logical or physical design stage. In the physical design stage the clustering of the entities may be done solely on the basis of performance considerations. The entity classes may be merged or split into different physical databases depending upon the access requirements.

The logical clustering of entity classes, i.e., assigning attributes to the entities, is dependent upon the inherent nature of the data and the data structure, whereas physical clustering is not. It is a necessary, but not sufficient, rule to say that attributes are clustered within an entity because they best identify that entity, and that entities are clustered into an entity model to satisfy a user's view of the data.

The logical clustering of entities is done to satisfy

- The data area involved
- The inherent data structure
- The local view of the user
- The queries against the data
- The data-processing needs of the user

The clustering of entities on the basis of data area means essentially that all data for which a department is responsible is clustered as that department's data. For example, all data for which the accounting department has a functional responsibility will be clustered as accounting data. Similarly, all data for which the personnel department has that responsibility will be clustered as personnel data.

The inherent data structure of an organization would indicate that employees are assigned to departments and to projects; that customers place orders; and that orders are for products. The clustering entities must reflect that inherent data structure. Both inherent data structure and the clustering reflect the business practices of the organization.

The clustering of entities on the basis of the local view of the user can be translated to mean that only those entities in which the user has some interest are assembled. The cluster may be part of a larger cluster or an amalgamation of several clusters. Thus, if the user wanted to determine the projects an employee worked on, the local view would consist of the attribute cluster of the employee and project entities.

The attributes within an entity and the clusterings of the entities must satisfy the queries made against them. For example, one could not answer a query about an employee's skills and education if these attributes were not in the entity. Similarly, a query about the percentage of an employee's time spent on a project would not be answered if there were no clustering of the employee and project entities and the relationship between them.

As in entity modeling, so in clustering entities the object of the exercise is to satisfy the data-processing needs of the user. The adequacy of the model is measured in relation to how well those needs are met. The entities will be clustered in accordance with those needs.

1.16 Application View and Logical Schema Design

An application view may be defined as the set of data which is required by that particular application to fulfill a specific data-processing need. For example, one application may be interested in materializing employee name and social security number as its employee entity, while another may materialize employee name, social security number, and salary as its employee entity. In turn, these two entities may be just a subset of a larger set of attributes which makes up a corporate or global entity called "employee entity."

We may have an application view of

- An entity class
- A cluster of entity classes
- A cluster of entity classes and physical databases
- A cluster of physical databases

The logical schema may be defined as the mapping of the entity model into the constructs provided by the database management system. An example is the mapping of the entity model into the DBMS package, information management system (IMS), a software package which allows the user to modify the stored data and provided by IBM.

In general, the logical schema indicates how the model will be stored and accessed. In the design of the logical schema, some reconstructing of the model, as well as changes to conform to the DBMS, may be necessary.

The entity model is not the logical schema.

- The entity model is a representation of the real-world view of the data.
- It is also the building blocks used for further data analysis and database design.
- The entity model is not restricted to any DBMS.
- Further, it is not directly implementable.

In short, the entity model serves as a stable framework or frame of reference into which new entities, attributes, and relationships can fit as more organizational database needs evolve.

1.17   Logical Schema—A Case Study

In this section I will construct a logical schema from the entity model shown in Figure 1.2. Because of space limitations, I will not create the schema for the entire model but will present a partial logical schema for Figure 1.4.

In the logical schema shown in Figure 1.5, note that the hierarchical data-structure concept of IMS is now applied to the entity model. We see that the pointers and unique keys are also imposed on the model.

If other relationships than those shown in the logical schema are required, these are shown, including all materialized attributes of relationships and their pointers.

The logical schema should also show the occurrences of the segments.

1.18   Logical and Physical Database Design

The process of developing a database structure from the users' requirements is called "database design." The database-design process consists of two phases:

- Design of a logical database structure (schema development) that is processable by the database management system and describes the user's view of the data
- Selection of a physical structure (physical database design) that is available within the DBMS

Four basic components are necessary to achieve a database-design methodology:

- A structural design process that consists of a series of design steps in which one alternative among many is chosen
- Design techniques for performing the required selection and evaluation of alternatives at each step
- Information requirements for input to the design process as a whole and to each step

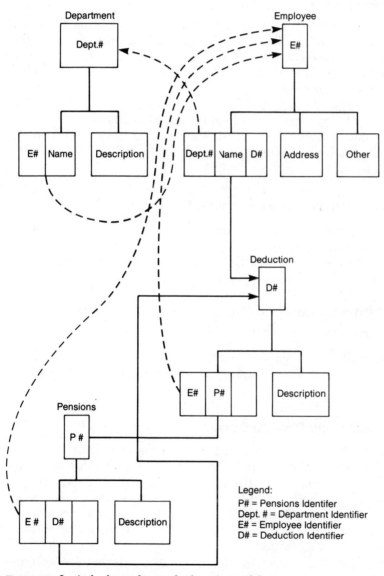

Figure 1.5 Logical schema for paycheck entity model

- A descriptive mechanism to represent the information input and the results at each design step

The result of the logical design step is a database definition or schema.

1.19 Formulating the DBMS—A Logical Database Schema

Using the entity-relationship diagrams developed during the users'-view modeling phase of database design, a processing matrix which links specific applications and entities identified in the processing requirements, and allowable DBMS characteristics, a logical database schema can be formulated.

In the simplest case, entities become record types and attributes become item types, or entities become logical databases.

In the more complex cases, entities can split or merge to form record types. This step begins the phase which requires consideration of the DBMS-specific rules and constraints.

1.20 Refining the Logical Database Schema

The logical database schema can now be revised on the basis of quantitative information and performance measures.

Performances measures at the logical design step are limited to:

- Logical record access counts
- Total bytes transferred to satisfy an application request
- Total bytes in the database

These measures attempt to predict physical database performance, in terms of elapsed time and physical storage space, as closely as possible.

1.21 Logical and Physical Design

Logical database design consists of integrating the requirements of a number of applications to arrive at a centrally controlled and maintained logical database structure. The central structure must support individual users' views of the data and support their processing needs. In order to store the database in a particular database environment, the structure should be defined in terms of the facilities, features, or constraints existing in that environment.

Physical database design involves evaluating alternatives for implementation of the logical database structure in a certain database environment, as well as choosing a storage structure, placement strategies, and searching mechanisms.

The three main phases of logical database design are as follows:

- *View modeling.* Using requirements specification as input, each user's view of the real world must be extracted and represented as explicitly as possible. The user's knowledge about the data and relationships at both schema and instance levels must be incorporated, and the effects of the processing of data upon these two levels must be considered.

- *View integration.* The several and possibly conflicting users' views must be integrated into one data model that represents a global view of the required data. The global model must support all users' views. The integration therefore entails merging individual views as well as making transformations.

- *Model optimization and mapping.* The model must first be analyzed and refined into an optimal structure. Then it must be matched against the logical structure available in an existing DBMS environment, and a database schema must be defined. Certain implementation-dependent alternatives are either analyzed in this phase or carried over into the physical database design.

The physical database design process maps the logical database structures into storage structures, taking into consideration the following factors.

- Data volume
- Access frequency and access path
- Selection of logical pointers and types of logical relationships
- Secondary indexing
- Trade-off between performance and redundancy
- Costs of controlling data redundancy
- Reorganization costs
- Recovery costs
- Initial load costs
- Operating-system access-method selections
- Physical storage media and placement selections
- Data-management access-method selections

Access-path design encompasses the logical ordering of records, pointer options, access methods, and overflow techniques.

Physical database design includes the identification of records to be placed in the same physical storage area and the allocation of records to secondary storage devices. It also includes the delineation of block size, buffer pool size, and data compression.

1.22   Documentation

Documentation is the recording of facts about objects or events of concern to facilitate communication and to provide a permanent record.

In a database environment, documentation is based on giving information about the database itself and about its contents and structure. The documentation focuses primarily on data-related components, such as

- Data elements
- Data groups, records, or segments
- Data structures
- Databases

Database documentation covers several types of information and is intended to support the needs of several classes of users. Seven types of documentation can be compiled for the database environment:

- *Name and meaning.*   A unique identifier and descriptive information that conveys the full meaning of the component. The name is used for reference and retrieval purposes, while the description is valuable to managers and users.
- *Physical description.*   The physical characteristic of the components, such as the size of a data element or the length of a data record.
- *Edit and authorization criteria.*   Criteria to be used to test the validity of instances of the component, such as the acceptable range of values for data elements, or passwords to allow the updating of a database.
- *Usage.*   Information on where and by whom or by what a component is used, such as the programs within a system that can reference a given data element.
- *Logical description.*   The characteristics and structure of each user's view of the database, such as logical relationships among data records.
- *Procedures.*   Guidelines for human interaction with the database, as during backup, recovery, and system restart.
- *Responsibility.*   A record of the individual or organizational unit responsible for the generation and maintenance of the database component.

1.23   Data Security and Integrity

Security is defined as the procedures and technical measures required (1) to prevent unauthorized access, modification of use, and dissemination of data stored or processed in a computer system, (2) to prevent any deliberate denial of service, and (3) to protect the system in its entirety from physical harm.

Security is normally divided into two areas of study: (1) physical security and (2) data security. *Physical security* is concerned with measures used to prevent physical access to computers, peripherals, and their surroundings. It includes providing identification to personnel for use in gaining access to computer rooms, locating computers away from heavily used areas, and installing tamperproof locks for computer rooms.

Data security is concerned with measures used to prevent access to stored data. Data security very often is concentrated on controlling access to stored data by providing passwords to authorized users and ensuring that those users are using only those resources for which permission was granted.

This access-control requirement is particularly important in time-shared and multiprogrammed systems in which multiple users are served concurrently. Jobs processed concurrently must be prevented from interfering with each other, and users must be prevented from gaining unauthorized access to each other's data or programs.

Privacy deals with the rights of individuals regarding the collection of information in a record-keeping system about their persons and activities, and with the processing, dissemination, storage, and use of this information in making determinations which affect the individuals concerned.

Integrity is a measure of the quality and reliability of the data on which computer-based information systems depend. Many computerized databases in use today suffer from high error rates in data they receive, and consequently they are riddled with bad data.

The major error problem lies in data that arrive at the computer already corrupted. The possible reasons for this corruption are manifold—human error in initial recording or formatting of data; faulty transcription of the data by either a human or a machine; accidentally lost, forgotten, or delayed data; deliberately falsified or omitted data; and the full range of other possible causes. It is also useful to include in our notion of erroneous data those cases in which no error has occurred in the transcription or transmission of the data, but rather in which the data faithfully represents an illegal or impossible event. That is, the error is not in the data, but in the information it conveys.

1.24   Threat and Risk Analyses

Threat and risk analyses are conducted to determine the level of
security and protection mechanisms in existence in an environment,
and the dangers to which the environment is exposed.

Threat analysis is defined as the methodology employed to assess the
level of the system's security and the protection mechanisms in place
to counter threats. It is also useful in designing a cost-effective security
system.

The methodology most frequently used and employed in threat-
analysis studies is the checklist or survey. This approach consists
essentially of a series of questions asked to determine what protection
measures are in place to counter threats against specific objects.

In one such study I conducted, the specific objects included

- Data dictionary
- Source and object modules for programming languages
- Source and object modules for program-development facilities
- Data files
- Message-processing programs
- Program specification block (PSB) library

The survey sought to determine what protection existed to counter
the following categories of threats:

- Unauthorized access to the libraries
- Unauthorized manipulation of the members of the libraries
- Authorized users browsing the library
- Unauthorized use of utility routines
- Inadequate auditing and monitoring of threats
- Illegal use of access privileges
- Destruction of storage medium
- Unauthorized distribution or exposure of reports
- Unauthorized copying or altering of libraries, programs, and reports
- Illegal deletion of stored data
- Passing of sensitive data by authorized users to unauthorized users
- Access to residues of data
- Unauthorized use of terminals
- Collusion of employees

- Denial of access to system resources
- Inadequate audit trials
- Inadequate training and education in security-related issues
- Attitude toward security-related issues
- Exposure of sensitive data following abnormal ending of jobs

Examples of the survey questions used to determine the protection mechanisms in place to counter the last threat in the above list are

- Does the computer give a dump of memory if an abnormal end of a job occurs during the running of a sensitive program?
- If the answer to the above question is "yes," who reviews these dumps and is responsible for their distribution?

The responses to the survey are then analyzed to determine if the protection mechanism, when present, is adequate or not. For example, some responses may reveal that there are

- Inadequate authentication of user identification
- Inadequate controls against access to source libraries
- Inadequate controls over the use of utilities and special-purpose programs
- Inability to identify terminals and users in the event of a breach of security

A risk assessment seeks to determine the likelihood that a specific threat against an object will succeed and the cost if that threat succeeds. The risk assessment accomplishes the following:

- Classifies the corporation's data
- Determines the probability of a specific threat's occurring
- Determines the socioeconomic effects which will result if someone's privacy is invaded
- Determines the level of protection required
- Allows a cost-benefits study before it is decided what protection features to implement

1.25 Management Reports

A quiet revolution is occurring in the data-processing industry. The computer era of the 1960s and 1970s is giving way to the information era of the 1980s. The emphasis on hardware and software of the computer era is shifting toward a focus on information management as we enter the first decade of the information age.

This difference in focus is significant because it emphasizes the quality and the value of the output of the computer in contrast to the emphasis on quantity which prevailed in the past.

Great strides have been made in improving the quality of these products, in increasing the productivity of the firm, and in developing more effective information systems and services in support of business activities.

A new breed of managers is emerging to direct this age of information explosion. These managers have accepted the notion that the top information executive's job encompasses much more than managing data-processing expenses. They realize that the new job definition must now include the following objectives:

- Ensuring the integration of data-processing, administrative processing, and office labor-productivity programs

- Instituting accounting, cost-control, and budgeting innovations that will subject all information systems' overhead activities to the disciplines traditionally applied to direct labor

- Subjecting office labor-automation programs to analyses comparable to those applied to all other forms of capital investment

- Conceiving organizational designs that will permit information to be handled as a readily accessible and easily priced commodity, rather than as a bureaucratic possession

- Installing and monitoring measurement methods that will protect improvements in productivity achieved by automation programs

These new managers must have access to the various management reports that will enable them to fulfill their roles as information-resource managers. These reports are needed to enable managers to make better decisions, to control their businesses better, and to have information at their fingertips when they need it. Many organizations are providing these reports to managers in the form of decision support systems (DSS). Most definitions of *DSS* include computer-supported tasks, from simple data retrieval through several levels of analysis and modeling to complex risk-assessment and optimization models.

The attraction of DSS is their ability to support the company's executive officers in strategic planning done both quickly and well. DSS act as change agents to motivate the organizations to move in the chosen strategic directions.

It is the belief of several workers in strategic planning that the most successful companies of the future will bridge the gap between information processing and corporate planning, because the computer will be an essential tool in executive management's quest for strategic information and in its selection of strategic success factors.

The merger of strategic planning and information processing in the 1990s will finally create the environment in which strategic planning's full potential can be realized.

1.26 User and Information Center Requirements

A fairly recent phenomenon of information processing and information resource management is the concept of end-user computing and information centers.

End-user computing is a concept that makes users more and more responsible for the retrieval and processing of their own data. Some user-friendly tools are now available for users who do not have a tremendous amount of expertise with the data-processing tool. For example, fourth-generation languages are now available which do not require users to have any expertise in programming in order to retrieve data from a database.

An information center is a group of data-processing professionals with expertise in several technical areas formed within an organization to offer consulting, training, and technical assistance in the application of end-user computing tools. Such a center is a source of support for clients seeking information from many places with the aid of computing tools.

1.27 Information Center Case Study

A very good example of an information center was described by Johnson.[1] The center was set up about 3 years ago for a large oil company in New York. The center's singular goal is to support end-user computing. This means that the center is customer-oriented and attempts to accommodate its services to its customers' business environment. Except for training, all services are offered on call during normal working hours. And even training is provided as soon as a class can be formed rather than on a fixed schedule.

The center provides consultation, training, and technical assistance to all levels of the headquarters staff. Consulting includes discussions to determine if an application is suitable for end-user computing, and, if so, how best to incorporate it. Sufficient training is provided to make clients comfortable with a tool or procedure without transforming them into technical experts. The term "technical assistance" encompasses a broad range of on-call services aimed at keeping the client functioning and productive in computer access.

---

[1] R. T. Johnson, "The Infocenter Experience," *Datamation*, January 1984.

1.28   The Information Center's Services

The center's services include management overviews; consulting on applications, justification, tool selection, security, and control; equipment ordering on behalf of the client; equipment setup; training; technical assistance; and limited equipment trouble shooting and maintenance. The center also provides advice to employees on the purchase of microcomputers for home use.

Because of its size and purpose, the center does not write applications for its clients; that would not facilitate end-user computing. And although the center's services are available on call, there is a 4-hour limit on consultation or technical assistance per application, to ensure that no single user monopolizes the center.

When clients come to the center for advice on a new application, a team member discusses the problem with them and evaluates how best to handle their needs. For straightforward applications, the center's member simply recommends an approach or tool. For more complex problems, a second member is usually called in to help. If the application is complex enough to require contracting for conventional development by systems professionals, the client is directed to the appropriate people in other parts of the organization.

To help ensure consistency and accuracy in consultations, the center's team meets once a week to compare notes on significant recommendations. This meeting also enhances the team's education, while preventing any one member from overselling the tool that he or she normally supports.

1.29   Course Contents and Offerings of the Information Center

Training is geared to clients' schedules. Courses are also designed to give a working knowledge of tools without turning clients into technical experts. Each course maximizes hands-on student exercises and minimizes lecture sessions, and no course is longer than 1 day.

The center standardizes course content instead of tailoring it for each class, to ensure that all key points are covered. This policy also allows another member of the team to take over a class at any time.

The center supports a mixture of mainframe and microcomputer tools. The microcomputer is viewed as both inevitable and valuable. It is also viewed as a workstation, and not a stand-alone box. The standard workstation for professionals or managers consists of a microcomputer with 512K memory, a color monitor, a 3278 interface, and a modem. Clients are taught to use the microcomputer alone for small problems, and as a terminal connected to the mainframe for larger ones.

Software has been selected to provide similar functions on both the mainframe and the microcomputer. Generally, these functions are analysis and modeling, database query and report writing, graphics, and communications.

The center does not have the authority to dictate which tools to use. To provide thorough support, however, the center must limit its tool set to a manageable size.

1.30 Staffing the Information Center

The people who compose a client-support center must be top performers with excellent interpersonal and communications skills. Because of the fast-paced nature of the job, they must also be self-starters and good organizers who can juggle many tasks at once. To act as consultants, they should have experience both in the computing tools that they support and in general business practices. Moreover, team members should complement one another in skills and knowledge of business techniques. For example, the team should have expertise in database management systems and query, database applications, financial analysis and modeling, and microcomputers.

1.31 Problems Affecting the Information Center

One of the biggest initial problems affecting the information center described by Johnson was the fact that other computing professionals lacked an understanding of its role and impact upon the computing organization. Suddenly a new "upstart" unit was competing with the traditional computer-application developers and, even worse, was fast becoming the initial point of contact within the computing department for a majority of clients. Recommendations were being made to clients without any regard for conventional development work being done by the rest of the organization.

This situation was particularly troublesome to the staff members known as "functional coordinators," senior people who have insight into a business function such as controlling or refining.

Once the problem was identified, the center devised three ways to help ease the friction. The first was to educate the computing department about end-user computing. The goal was to assure functional coordinators and line managers that the center dealt only with computing tasks that could be accomplished without professional systems analysis and programming. In fact, it was pointed out, the center would be a help to the traditional organization by identifying additional users in need of computing services.

Second, the center coordinator scheduled regular meetings with computing managers and functional coordinators to keep everyone informed and up to date.

Finally, the center established guidelines for how and when it or the rest of the computing applications-development organization dealt with clients. Creating a log of the center's contacts with clients, which included a brief description of each meeting and any actions taken, was central to improving communication between the center and other departments.

1.32   Data Administration and Database Administration

Data administration (DA) is defined as the establishment and enforcement of policies and procedures for managing the company's data as a corporate resource. It involves the collection, storage, and dissemination of data as a globally administered and standardized resource.

Database administration (DBA) is a technical function which performs database design and development, provides education on database technology, provides support to users in operational data-management-related activities, and may provide technical support for data administration.

1.33   Establishing the Data-Administration Function

The need for the data-administration function in organizations arose for two main reasons:

- Organizations established database environments, purchased database management systems and software, and then discovered that they needed technical management to find solutions to the resulting problems.

- In recent years organizations have begun to recognize data as a valuable resource requiring expert management. They have come to realize that the required management can be best obtained by setting up data administration departments.

Before a data-administration function can be established, certain conditions must exist:

- Top management must be willing to take a long-range view of the cost structure.

- Data processing and line management must be prepared for the database approach, with its associated protocols and standards.

- The entire line management must view data as a resource similar to raw materials, equipment, finance, and personnel.

The initiative in establishing a data-administration function can originate anywhere in the data-processing organization. However, the most common starting point for the idea is a data-processing professional who becomes concerned about the growing demands for the proper administration and management of the organization's data resources. On the other hand, there are times when top management focuses on the data-resource issue before the data-processing professionals do. This usually occurs when management becomes aware of the need to manage data as a resource, or experiences a lack of information supporting a planning or decision-making process.

The establishment of the data-administration function is fast becoming a critical decision for most organizations. It is a very important area of data management, and once the decision is made to establish the function, everyone charged with that decision should ensure that top management not only supports the decision but becomes involved in the ongoing functioning of the DA department.

1.34 The Functions of Data Administration

Data administration serves to provide custody of the organization's data and coordinate data activities with systems developers and users.

The data-administration functions will include

- Logical design of database systems
- Liaison with systems personnel during the applications-development process
- Training all relevant personnel in data-administration concepts and techniques
- Setting and monitoring data-management standards
- Design of documentation, including data dictionaries
- Promoting and allowing for interdepartmental data sharing
- Resolution of data-sharing conflicts
- Setting up facilities to monitor data-usage authorization

1.35 The Activities of Data Administration

The functions defined in the above section are achieved through certain activities by data administration. These activities may or may not be carried out in all DA departments, but those which are classified as successful must undertake to carry out several or all of them.

The development and enforcing of policies governing data collection must rank as the most important activity conducted by DA. Other activities include

- Developing tactical and strategic plans for data
- Developing definitional requirements for data dictionary items
- Developing and enforcing naming conventions
- Identifying potential database applications
- Planning the evolution of the organization's database

1.36   Functions of Database Administration

Database administration is concerned with the technical aspects of managing the data resource within the organization, rather than with the administration aspects. Managing those technical aspects requires expertise in a particular database management system and in designing database logical and physical structures.

The DBA functions include

- Physical design of database systems
- Assisting in the negotiation for the acquisition of hardware and software to support the database management system
- Acting as a contact point for users who have problems with the DBMS and associated software
- Monitoring the performance of the DBMS and the individual transactions against the databases
- Assisting in the development of long-term plans to ensure that adequate hardware capacity and facilities are available to meet the requirements of new systems, or expansions of existing systems

1.37   Standards and Naming Conventions

The importance of data-processing standards in an organization cannot be overemphasized. A set of standards can be a powerful productivity technique. Standards are simply a guide to what has been successful in the past and thus will tend to ensure success in the future. They can also be an effective way to ensure consistency and communication between data-processing professionals and users.

Data-processing standards, system standards, and programming standards are but three of the installation standards that should be present in an organization.

Data-processing standards cover the operation and control of computers, whether they are in a mainframe data center under management control or in minicomputers or microcomputers in users' locations.

Systems standards cover the various phases of the project life cycle, from the initial business-information-planning process through the steps of system proposal, functional design, detailed design, programming, conversion, and postaudit. A technical appendix might include detailed guidelines concerning interviewing techniques for data gathering and analysis, cost-benefits analyses, project-estimating techniques, package program search and evaluation steps, structured design methodology, documentation standards, and general control standards.

Programming standards must be unique to each organization, but might include standard naming conventions; the languages used, including the preferred procedure; program cataloguing procedures; access-control methods; job-control language (JCL) standards; printing specifications for different printers; description of standard subroutines; software aids; the tools and utilities in use; and debugging tips.

The centralization of data into an integrated shared database promises to reduce redundancy and improve data consistency. To achieve these benefits requires that the content of the database be clear and unambiguous to all those who interact with it. Standards that govern the naming of data elements can improve communication among database users and can catch redundancy or inconsistency before it becomes part of the database.

1.38 Change Control

Changes are part of the evolutionary process of any database environment. The control of changes is a critical activity in this environment. This control is necessary for three reasons:

- To preserve the integrity of the data and maintain existing security standards
- To ensure that changes are communicated to all affected users
- To determine the impact of those changes

In the database environment the control of change activity is the domain of the data administration department. The DA department must define standards and procedures indicating who can make changes, the level of changes that can be made, and the documentation that should be prepared to communciate those changes.

The DA department, through the use of the data dictionary, must document how these changes are going to be communicated to the affected users. This can often be accomplished by keeping an inventory of the occurrence of certain items destined for change, the programs that use these items, the data accessed by these programs, and the various users of the data.

1.39 Hardware and Software Performance Statistics

In selecting the logical structure and physical implementation for a database, the DA must strike a delicate balance. For each application, different structures and storage methods yield different cost-performance results. The DA must weigh these trade-offs and select the configuration that produces the best overall performance for the least cost.

The DA must be constantly aware of the database performance and alert to signs of imbalance. In order to do this the DA must be familiar with the causes of imbalance and their effects on performance. Measures must be developed and used regularly to detect performance problems and to guide the DA in improving the performance of the database.

The cost-performance balance of a database environment can be upset if the hardware configuration is inadequate or underutilized. Inadequate or heavily loaded secondary storage devices can bog down system throughput by requiring extensive searches for free space. The DA department must be in a position to resolve hardware performance imbalances.

Performance problems can also be the result of factors related to system software, including the DBMS itself. Improper memory management and resource management can also contribute to performance problems.

The DA can assist in resolving these problems by setting standards for buffer sizes, coding, choice of algorithms for accessing the database, and overflow methods.

1.40 Consistency Checks

In the database environment the ability to validate data items is of the utmost importance. Because the tremendous amounts of data stored in the databases very often make it difficult to maintain the quality of the data, the consistency checks and validation rules in the database environment should be adequate.

The consistency checks should address errors that may occur in data item names and values. They should indicate ranges of data values and the action to be taken if these values exceed the prescribed range.

Consistency checks should also include checks for reasonableness, and when applied to data items, the checks should identify values which are unreasonable and state what further investigation should be carried out in this case.

In applying consistency checks to data items, one should be able to determine the impact of changes in the set of acceptable values which can be assumed by the data items. The actions necessary to update acceptable values of other related data items should also be described.

Consistency checks should be viewed as part of the database integrity controls to ensure that changes in the set of acceptable data values are propagated to other related data values whose value sets are also affected.

1.41   Summary

This chapter discussed the basic concept of data dictionaries and the environments in which data dictionaries are used.

The *dictionary* was defined as an organized reference to the data content of an organization's programs, systems, databases, collections of files, and manual records.

The environments in which the dictionary is used were given detailed coverage but limited primarily to those with database-related operating systems.

2

Concepts of
Data Dictionaries

Introduction

This chapter discusses various concepts of data dictionaries. It indicates what a dictionary is, the concept of metadata, and active versus passive data dictionaries, and it outlines several actual uses of data dictionaries in large corporations.

2.1   What Is a Data Dictionary?

The *data dictionary* was defined in Chapter 1 as an organized reference to the data content of an organization's programs, systems, databases, collections of all files, or manual records.

The data dictionary may be maintained manually or by a computer. Sometimes the term "data dictionary" refers to a software product that is utilized to maintain a dictionary database. The data dictionary will contain names, descriptions, and definitions of the organization's data resources.

2.2   The Concept of Metadata

In the broadest sense, a data dictionary is any organized collection of information about data.

In the real world, any information system, whether or not it is computerized, exists to store and process data about objects (entities). We then create data records to represent occurrences of these entities. We define specific record types to represent specific entity types. Frequently, we also assign keys or identifiers, such as customer names and invoice numbers, to differentiate one record occurrence from another. A data dictionary can then be designed to contain data about those customer and invoice record types.

The customer and invoice records in the database contain ordinary data. The record in the data dictionary contains metadata, or data about the data. For example, the record in the data dictionary may contain the name, the record length, the data characteristics, and the recording mode of the record in the database.

2.3   Active versus Passive Data Dictionaries

Data dictionaries are often categorized as active or passive. This refers to the extent of their integration with the database management systems. If the dictionary and the DBMS are integrated to the extent that the DBMS uses the definitions in the dictionary at run time, the dictionary is active. If the dictionary is freestanding or independent of the DBMS, it is passive.

An active dictionary must contain an accurate, up-to-date description of the physical database in order for the database management system to access the data.

In a passive dictionary environment more effort is required to keep two copies of the same data, and great care must be taken to ensure that the two copies are actually identical.

2.4   Case Histories of Data Dictionary Use

Company A is a large leading energy company in New York City. This company's database administration department has been evolving since 1976. The stated objectives of DBA are as follows.

- Data is an important shared resource that, like other major corporate resources, should be managed and controlled.
- Knowledge of how data and information are generated and used should be widely disseminated.
- Control should be exercised over the quality of the data resource, to increase its effective utilization.

The DBA function exerts control over the data resources through management control of application, development, testing, and production environments. The company's DBA function sees its proper role as a full-time participant in the planning, design, and operation of database systems, with a view to ensuring that adequate features and appropriate data safeguards are provided.

In all these efforts, managers of database administration see the data dictionary as the primary tool for their functions. The data dictionary is being used to organize the collection, storage, and retrieval of information about data.

2.5 Data Dictionary Use at Company A

The facilities of company A data dictionary are useful to all systems-development projects, nondatabase as well as database. The main thrust is to capture information describing data items and their attributes, highlighting their interrelationships. Functional analysis is also supported by the dictionary, based on its ability to define business activities in a machine-readable form.

The data dictionary is a tool which enables the DBA function to

- Clarify and design data structures
- Avoid unwanted data redundancies
- Generate accurate and dependable data definitions
- Assess the impact of proposed computer system changes
- Enforce standards related to data

Because of the interest in management uses of data, the DBA function attempts to determine what management-type data can be provided by each new applications system. The DBA introduces appropriate integrated database designs that minimize the need for special processing to make data suitable for current and future management uses.

2.6 An Example of Management Uses of the Data Dictionary

An example of management use of the data dictionary is the human resources information system (HURIS). Now under development, this system will establish a single source of data about people within the company, servicing such application functions as payroll, employee relations, and benefit plans. In addition to the ongoing review function and assistance in database design and installation, the DBA function developed a control monitor that supports an unusually flexible security apparatus, as well as an online report request and distribution system for end users.

2.7 Company A's Approach to Using the Data Dictionary

The first step in company A's approach to using the data dictionary was to acquire the basic dictionary capabilities and train the DBA staff member in their use. Then corporate policies were established that required dictionary use for all database projects. The DBA is now in the process of developing additional tools, procedures, and educational materials to enhance the usefulness of the data dictionary.

Ultimately, the DBA function must impose a discipline on data content and not just its form. The staff must coordinate the definition of all data that crosses departmental boundaries; for data that is used only by one department, there is less need to impose standards. The DBA function needs to clean up the existing data definitions and then monitor all additions, deletions, and changes to these definitions.

In the long run, the monitoring and editing of data definitions are essential if data resources are to become truly shareable. The editing of key data definitions found in all application systems is a very large undertaking, so this step should be approached somewhat cautiously.

2.8 Company A's Use of the Data Dictionary for Business Planning

An area of current interest is the mechanism by which the DBA function can support business planning. Beginning with the business objectives, the business processes needed to support these objectives are identified and recorded in the dictionary. Next, the information needs of those business processes, which support the locating of data-sharing opportunities, are identified and recorded in the dictionary. All this data—concerning business opportunities, processes, information, and sharing potential—can be made more manageable in the context of a data dictionary.

These planning processes have not yet been fully realized at company A. The DBA's own understanding of these methods must be developed, and the corporate community must be educated about the advantages of the formal definitions of information entities.

Company A has thus embarked on a broad program for the management and control of its data resources.

2.9 Data Dictionary Use at Company B

Company B is a large telephone company in a large Canadian city. This company's data-administration department has been evolving since 1977.

Company B has had the online IBM data dictionary for several years, but is not making extensive use of its capabilities. The data-administration area uses the dictionary as a passive tool to maintain details of the database control blocks, database definitions, and program-specification blocks. The dictionary facilitates the management of several test and production versions of database definitions. The company has captured some descriptions of major databases and files and their fields, but has not progressed to the point of describing in detail all major databases and files.

The company reported that the IBM dictionary is not particularly user-friendly and has been relegated, almost solely, to use by technical database-support personnel. The company's information center personnel did not find the dictionary easy to use, and found that the standard reports produced were somewhat lacking in user appeal. They found that the screens used for input and query were not, however, easily changed and were definitely geared to more technical users than those which the information center supports.

2.10 Company B's Use of the Extensibility Feature of the Data Dictionary

The extensibility features of the IBM data dictionary allow the user to code, debug, and document development systems and their programs. Entire batch or online transaction-driven system can be developed using the extensibility features. However, company B is not currently using these features.

The company is currently involved in the production of a corporate data model. Data administration is now considering placing the results of the data model into the extensibility categories in the dictionary, as the data-model results are of prime importance to the management of data within the corporation.

According to company B, no one dictionary on the market handles the areas of production-control block and data-definition program code, the data-analysis by-products, and the database-design assistance requirements well enough to be the sole tool used in those areas. For these reasons, the data dictionary at company B is not used extensively.

2.11 The Metadata Entries for a Typical Dictionary

In order to manage data as a resource that is shared by users at all levels in an organization, it is essential that data about data—metadata—be clearly specified, easily accessible, and well controlled. The first step in this process is to identify and describe those data objects that are of interest to the organization and about which the organization wishes to store information. The data used to identify and describe the objects is entered into the data dictionary system as metadata.

Metadata should not be confused with the user data or actual data that is stored in the dictionary. For example, the metadata for an attribute "customer name" will describe the entry for that attribute as "the name of a person who conducts business with the organization," whereas the user data will give the name of the customer, e.g., "Tom Clark."

An example of the metadata for an attribute in the data dictionary follows.

- *Attribute name.* A symbolic or descriptive name conventionally used to identify the attribute and its representations. Attribute names are used as the preferred method of referencing attributes

- *Aliases.* A list of names used as alternate identifiers for the attribute and its representations.

- *Attribute description.* A freeform narrative containing a description of the attribute and its various representations. The description contains a concise definition of the attribute in a form suitable for use in a glossary.

- *Attribute function.* A freeform narrative describing the corporate interest in the attribute and its physical representations. The narrative describes the purpose and usage of the attribute as it relates to corporate objectives and the business functions used to achieve them.

- *Definition update source.* A composite structure identifying the individuals or groups who updated a dictionary entry and the dates on which those updates were made. A single occurrence of the structure is recorded for each update. It takes the form "source (date)," where "source" is a 3-character field identifying the person or group who submitted the definition modification.

- *Definition acceptance status.* A composite structure identifying the project teams or organizational groups who created the definition or who must be informed of its subsequent updates. The structure is used as the basis for propagating definition changes to support groups who may be affected by the proposed modifications.

- *Definition responsibility.* A set of references to the organizational groups charged with the responsibility for the accuracy and ongoing integrity of a definition. The references are used to establish a relationship between the dictionary entry and the organizational groups identified as the definitive source of information about the attribute's meaning and use.

- *Standard representation entries.* A composite structure listing the physical characteristics of the representation defined as the standard representation of attribute values.

Standard representatives attributes are documented in the following form:

```
STANDARD REPRESENTATION ATTRIBUTES
JUSTIFICATION         -   LEFT
CODING STRUCTURE      -   ALPHABETIC
DATA LENGTH           -   10 CHARACTERS
SCALE FACTOR          -   1000
NUMERIC TYPE          -   INTEGER
NUMERIC PRECISION     -   6 DIGITS
NUMERIC VALUE         -   NEGATIVE
STORAGE FORMAT        -   BINARY
RECORDING MODE        -   FIXED
STORAGE LENGTH        -   3 BYTES
```

- *Access authority.* A set of references to the organizational groups within the company who have the right to grant access to attribute values.

- *Authorized users.* A set of references to the organizational groups who have been granted access privileges to the information represented by the attribute and its physical representations. The references identify who uses the attribute and whether or not they can create, delete, or modify attribute values.

- *Value set assignment responsibility.* A set of references to the organizational groups who have the right to add to, delete from, or otherwise modify the set of acceptable values which can be assumed by the attribute values.

- *Entity class membership.* A reference to the *entity class* which includes the attribute as a component. The name must identify an entity class defined elsewhere in the dictionary.

- *Logical group membership.* A list of names identifying the *logical groups* which include the attribute as component. The names in the list must correspond to the names associated with *logical group definitions* recorded elsewhere in the dictionary.

- *Logical record membership.* A list of names identifying the *logical records containing physical* representations of the attribute. The names included in the list must correspond to the names associated with *logical record definitions* recorded elsewhere in the dictionary.

- *Validity and edit rules.* A freeform narrative listing the edit rules which must be satisfied by attribute values stored in groups, segments, or similar physical data structures. The narrative includes syntactical rules dictating the format or internal structure of the attribute values.

- *Consistency checks.* A freeform narrative listing the consistency checks which must be satisfied by all attribute values. The narrative includes tables defining value correlations between related attributes.

- *Reasonableness checks.* A narrative listing the reasonableness checks which, when applied against attribute values, identify values which are reasonable and should be further investigated. The narrative includes tables identifying acceptable subsets of attribute values and the circumstances in which those restricted subsets apply.

- *Usage propagation.* A freeform narrative describing the impact of changes made to attribute values held in physical data structures and the steps which must be taken to propagate the changes throughout the database.

- *Validation Propagation.* A freeform narrative describing the impact of changes in the set of acceptable values which can be assumed by an attribute, and the action necessary to update the acceptable values of other related attributes. The narrative includes the names of attributes whose acceptable values can be affected by the changes.

2.12   The Data Dictionary as a Directory

"Data directory" is another term that is frequently used. As a rule, a dictionary gives the descriptions and definitions of an organization's data, whereas the directory gives the storage location of that data. However, many software vendors use these terms interchangeably; although some consistently use one or the other.

A data dictionary may contain a lot more than the location of stored data. It may be considered to be a machine-readable definition of a computerized database. It is often used by a database management system to obtain the sizes, formats, and locations of data records and fields. A data dictionary may be considered a superset that can contain additional data and definitions. Some vendors of database management systems now use the term "catalog" instead of "directory" or "dictionary." This usually means that the system includes a repository of metadata which is more extensive than the usual directory but not so elaborate as a dictionary.

2.13   Maintenance of the Data Dictionary

The most important reason for the existence of a data dictionary is its ability to produce reports that are accurate and timely. For this reason the maintenance of an organization's data dictionary is a very critical issue.

The maintenance of the data dictionary should be carried out in the following areas:

- The definitive information
- Propagation effects and control of changes
- Access authorization of users
- Consistency and validation checks
- Directory and data-storage features
- Relationship and membership of entry
- Environmental data

The definitive information of the data dictionary will include the naming convention, the description and function of the entry, who is responsible for the definition and any subsequent update, and the data representation of the definition. Any maintenance carried out on the entries will ensure that the definitive information is correct and always reflects the current status in both accuracy and timeliness.

Any change in the data dictionary contents should be made only after the effect of that change is evaluated. The person responsible for changes should determine which users, which programs and systems, and which relationships' cross-references will be affected. Ideally, all changes should be done from one central terminal or controlled by one central organization. Unauthorized or unapproved changes should never be allowed in the dictionary environment.

2.14   Access Authorization of Users

The data dictionary should always contain accurate and timely information on the access authorization of all users. This information should include not only access to the data dictionary itself but also access to the stored data. Any change in access authorization of a user should be immediately shown in the dictionary, and appropriate measures should be taken to maintain the existing data-security level.

2.15   Consistency and Validation Checks

Because of the multiple origins of names and definitions in the data dictionary, the number of inconsistencies in the names is often very high. Some organizations attempt to cut down on these inconsistencies by having several versions of the project data dictionary, with one dictionary designated as the corporate dictionary. Names and definitions are moved to the corporate dictionary only when it is established that no changes will be made in the entry. Thus the need for maintenance of the corporate dictionary seldom arises.

2.16   Directory and Data-Storage Features

One function of the data dictionary is to act as a directory or pointer to the stored data or to the metadata. The dictionary may contain unique identifiers which will allow the user to determine the location of the metadata formats. For example, in a particular data dictionary developed in-house, the metadata was stored on seven volumes of disk storage. Each category of the definition carried an entry called "library identifier." This identifier took the form XXXNNNNN, where XXX was a 3-character alphabetic field identifying the volume containing the definition, and NNNNN was a 5-character numeric field which served as a unique identifier within a volume.

A user wishing to access the dictionary definitions needs only to code the library identifier in the job-control language if running in a batch mode, or to enter the identifier when required to do so if running in an interactive mode.

2.17   Relationship or Membership of an Entry

A very important feature of the data dictionary is its ability to show relationships between an attribute and the record to which it belongs, a file and its database, and a database and its logical schema. It is very important that these relationships be properly maintained. During update or deletion activities these linkages must be maintained.

2.18   Environmental Data

Many data dictionaries contain entries describing the operating environment of the organization. For example, the entries may indicate whether a traditional operating environment or a database environment is used.

Other dictionaries may indicate the storage media for stored data or metadata. The maintenance aspect of data dictionaries must account for any change in the operating environment.

2.19   Active and Passive Data Dictionaries

Dictionaries are generally classified into one of two categories: (1) active and (2) passive.

A dictionary in the passive mode is used mainly as a repository of information on attributes, records, files, databases, and schemas. A user wanting access to this information may go to a shelf and retrieve this information from the dictionary, or retrieve it from a computer if the dictionary is computerized.

A dictionary in the active mode may be used in conjunction with the operating system to lock out unauthorized users from stored data or metadata. For example, the dictionary may contain an authorization table showing the names of users and the data they are authorized to access. A request from a user is channeled to the data dictionary, and access authorization is determined. If the request is legitimate, access to the data is granted. If the request exceeds the authorization, the request is denied and an audit trail for post facto analysis is created.

In the active mode a data dictionary can be used for the automated design of databases. This feature is very often difficult to implement, and its use may still be several years in the future for most organizations.

2.20   Design of Data Dictionaries

The next chapter will discuss in detail the design of data dictionaries. This section will serve to introduce the design of a basic data dictionary.

Data dictionaries are designed to give definite information about the objects in which an organization may have an interest. The entries in the dictionary may include attributes, entities, records, files, and databases.

The typical entries for an attribute will include, among others, the name, any aliases, the description and function, data length, origin of definition of attribute, validity, update authorization, security, and consistency checks.

In addition to the above, the design should include features for accessing and retrieving from the dictionary.

2.21   Control and Audit Features of Data Dictionaries

A data dictionary can be used as a tool to control access to an organization's data. It can also be used by internal or external auditors to monitor the data-security effort of an organization.

In the area of controls, the data dictionary can be used to control changes to attributes, entities, or files. By including in the dictionary the names of those responsible for making changes, the organization can limit this activity to authorized individuals.

The dictionary can also be used to control the effects that changes would have on users, programs, and applications. If the names of those affected by changes are included, organization can immediately notify those affected.

A dictionary can be used in both the active and passive modes to control access, not only to metadata but also to the stored data. An access-authorization table contained in the dictionary can be used to control access to data.

Internal auditors can use the data dictionary during systems development to ensure that agreed-upon standards are being adhered to by systems designers. They can use it to audit naming conventions and standards, and to determine who are authorized users of the system and their authorization levels.

The data dictionary can be used in an active mode to interface with the operating system to produce audit trails to analyze attempts made by users to breach the organization's security.

2.22 Data Dictionary Standards

Data dictionary standards may fall into any of the following categories:

- Metadata contents
- Interface with external environment
- Interface with command languages
- Access rules and control
- Customized and management reports
- Security
- Interrelations between entries
- Extensibility

Standards in metadata contents would clearly indicate which entries should be found in the dictionary. For example, the standard entry for an attribute should include name, function, description, alias, definition responsibility, standard representation, edit rules, and access-control features.

A dictionary design should include standards for interfacing with the external environment. In this regard the standards may be as simple as including an entry describing the physical environment and its operating system, or as complex as using the data dictionary to control access to the stored data and the operating system itself.

Standards for interfacing with command languages indicate how high-level languages, such as Fortran and PL1, will use the data dictionary to build file structures and layouts, and how retrieval languages will access the data dictionary itself.

Standards for access rules and control indicate who can access the dictionary, how the dictionary contents would be accessed, and whether the contents would be accessed in its original form or in the form of copies of the data.

Standards in the area of security cover the security of the data dictionary and its contents, and security techniques for protecting the external environment.

Standards indicating the interrelationships between entries show how an attribute is related to a group, record, file, or database. In reverse order, the standards show what attributes comprise the database, entity, or file.

Standards in the area of extensibility indicate what features can be included by users and how users can enhance the dictionary capability or make it more user-friendly.

Chapter 9 is devoted to data dictionary standards and discusses this topic in greater detail.

2.23   The Data Dictionary as a Tool for Data Analysis

Data analysis is defined as documenting the entities in which the organization has an interest. It is in this area that the data dictionary is most useful. In data analysis the organization attempts to determine the entities and the role they play. The data dictionary can be used to record this information. The dictionary can not only give definitive information about the entities but also describe the relationships between the entities and how these entities can be used to model the organization's data environment.

During data analysis, inconsistencies, redundancies, and incompleteness in the data are determined. A source for such determinations is the data dictionary.

Again, during data analysis the development teams may want to determine the originators of a definition, whether the definition has homonyms or synonyms, and the aliases by which the definition may be identified. The dictionary should supply information to answer these queries.

Finally, the entries (metadata) in the data dictionary serve as a useful guideline or standard that can be followed by the data analyst who wishes to document information about attributes, entities, and relationships in an efficient and structured manner.

3

Design of In-House Data Dictionaries

Introduction

More and more organizations are increasingly turning to their own resources to develop data dictionaries in-house to meet their own requirements.

Surveys I conducted of the Fortune 500 and the Financial Post 500 companies revealed some dissatisfaction with current data dictionaries supplied by manufacturers of computer hardware. Many users found it difficult to adapt the dictionaries to their unique environments, others found that several features used as selling points for the manufacturers' dictionaries were inoperable and years away from being useful in their organizations, and still others found that the dictionaries were not useful in helping them to model the business functions of their organization.

The intent of this chapter is to describe some approaches that will be useful to an organization thinking about developing its own data dictionary system. The major portion of the chapter will describe one approach to designing data dictionaries: the entity-relationship approach.

3.1 The Entity-Relationship Approach

Database design using the entity-relationship (ER) model begins with a list of the entity types involved and the relationships among them. This approach assumes that the designer knows what the entity types are at the outset. The entity-relationship approach asserts that one of the results of systems analysis is a clear understanding of the entities involved.

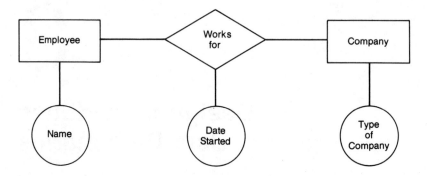

Figure 3.1   The entity-relationship diagram

The ER approach uses entity-relationship diagrams, as illustrated in Figure 3.1. In this figure the rectangular boxes represent entity types, the diamond-shaped box represents a relationship between entities, and the circular figures represent attributes.

During the data-analysis phase of database design, the analysts try to discover all the entities that are required to solve the problem as stated during the problem-definition phase. These entities, their attributes, and the relationships among them are recorded in the data dictionary as they are discovered.

The result of the data-analysis phase is an entity model, giving a diagrammatical representation of the entities and their relationships. The entity model is translated into a logical schema—a diagrammatical representation of entities with the constructs of the particular database management system superimposed. The logical schema is in turn translated into the physical databases required to satisfy the user's requirement.

It is important to note that all the above phases of database design are carefully documented in the data dictionary. The next few sections will describe a data dictionary developed to support databases built using the ER approach.

3.2   Introduction to the ER Data Dictionary

The ER data dictionary described here consists essentially of a set of definitions and entries for attributes, entity classes, logical schemas, and databases. The linkages between the various volumes which contain the definitions are maintained in the form of a set of pointers. Thus it is very simple to illustrate which attributes are members of which entity class, which entity classes make up the logical schemas, and which logical schemas are used to design the physical databases.

The data dictionary was developed in an environment which uses the IBM information management system and operating system (OS)

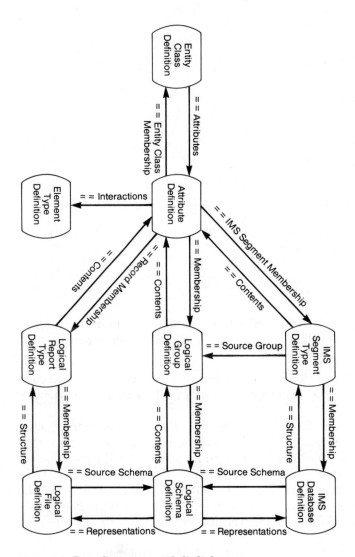

Figure 3.2 Data dictionary symbolic linkages

and therefore includes entries of IMS segments, OS logical records and files, and IMS databases.

However, because of the modular nature of the implementation, the data dictionary can be used with any database management system.

The data dictionary entries are established during the data-analysis phase of database design and become a very important input into the physical database design phase.

The data dictionary described here consists of nine components, as illustrated in Figure 3.2. These components are

- Attributes
- Data elements
- Entity classes
- IMS databases
- IMS segments
- Logical files
- Logical groups
- Logical records
- Logical schemas

The sections below describe these components and the extraction and retrieval programs in more detail.

3.3   Definitions and Terms Used in the Data Dictionary

The following definitions and terms, in addition to those already introduced in Chapters 1 and 2, are necessary in order to fully appreciate the uses of this dictionary.

1. *Access group.*   A physical clustering of attributes based on common usage, access requirements, and data-security or privacy requirements.

In a database environment using the IMS database management system, an access group could be attributes from one or more IMS segments or from one or more physical databases. This translates into a group taken from one or more entities.

The concepts of access groups in an IMS environment which uses the current retrieval language (DL/1) to retrieve segments is not readily accepted. However, many organizations are using routines written by users to retrieve access groups.

2. *Access statistics.*   Data collected about the frequency of retrieval of a particular stored attribute over a given period of time.

These statistics provide a means of making performance-oriented judgments when designing physical databases. In particular, these statistics assist in the choice of physical and logical parents and the left-to-right ordering of IMS segments. They are also useful in the selection of secondary indexes, since attributes that are updated frequently make poor target fields.

Access statistics can have a major effect on the placing of dependent segments in relation to their root and on the decision to combine segments in preference to decreasing data independence.

3.4   Structure of the Data Dictionary

Figure 3.2 illustrates the entire components of the data dictionary. In this figure the arrows represent components. For example, the attribute arrow between "entity class definition" and "attribute" indicates that the attribute is a component of that particular entity. The entity class membership arrow indicates that the attribute is a member of the particular entity.

Similarly, the IMS segment membership arrow indicates that the named attribute is a member of the particular IMS segment. The contents arrow indicates that the attribute is part of the listed attributes of the IMS segment.

The interactions arrow indicates that the attribute has the element type as its base unit or is derived from the element. The attribute is an element that plays a particular role in an organization. For example, "date" may be defined as an element. However, "start date" will be defined as an attribute, because it indicates the date an employee started with a company, for example. That is, it now assumes a role.

The entries of the nine components are primarily narrative information about the components. For example, the attribute definition entries include name, description, function, alias, data storage, update responsibility, and validity information.

These nine components will be discussed in this chapter and elsewhere in the book in more detail.

3.5   The Attribute Definition

An *attribute definition* is a category of entry in the data dictionary describing an entity "attribute" and its representations.

An *attribute* is defined as any property or characteristic of an entity which, individually or in combination with other attributes, provides a description or view of an entity tailored to a particular environment.

Attribute definitions describe both the coding schemas associated with an attribute and the role served by the attribute in relationship to its parent entity.

The components of an attribute definition include

1. The primary name and aliases used to reference the attribute verbally and in formal documentation

2. General descriptive information about the attribute and its role within the organization

3. Symbolic references used to locate the attribute definition within the data dictionary

4. The names of project teams and organizational groups with an ongoing interest in the definition and its updates

5. The names of organizational groups responsible for the ongoing accuracy and integrity of the definitions

6. References to corporate documentation associated with the attribute

7. Standard characteristics of the coding schema and data fields used to represent attribute values

8. The names of organizational groups who have the right to grant access to the units of information represented by attribute values

9. The names and access privileges of organizational groups who have been granted access rights to the attribute values

10. The names of organizational groups who can add to, delete from, or otherwise modify the set of acceptable values which can be assumed by an attribute

11. The names of the entity classes which include the attribute as a component

12. The names of logical groups, IMS segments, and logical records containing representations of the attribute

13. References to other entries in the data dictionary associated in some specified manner with the attribute

14. Edit rules, consistency checks, and checks for reasonableness which must be satisfied by all occurrences of an attribute

15. Instructions defining the action to be taken in propagating changes to attribute values in physical data structures

16. Instructions defining the actions to be taken in propagating changes to the sets of values which can be assumed by an attribute

The specifications defining the contents of an attribute definition are given in Figure 3.3.

The library entry identifier is an 8-character numeric field which serves as a unique identifier within a volume.

The attribute name is a symbolic or descriptive name used to identify the attribute and its representation.

"Aliases" is a list of names used as alternate identifiers for the attribute and its representations.

"Classification" is a descriptive code assigned to all data dictionary entries, identifying the type of definition. For an attribute definition, the classification takes the value "attribute definition" and is documented as follows:

```
= = CLASSIFICATION
     ATTRIBUTE DEFINITION
```

```
    a) External parameters
          library entry identifier
    b) Internal sections
 = = Name: attribute name
 = = ALIASES
     alias name 1 (  context or usage comments  )
     -----------------------------------------------
     alias name n (  context or usage comments  )
 = = CLASSIFICATION
       ATTRIBUTE DEFINITION
 = = DESCRIPTION
       attribute description
 = = FUNCTION
     1. attribute function 1
     ----------------------------
     n. attribute function n
 = = DEFINITION UPDATE SOURCE
       SOURCE 1 (data 1)
     ------------------
       SOURCE n (data n)
 = = USER ACCEPTANCE STATUS
       status code 1, group 1
     ------------------------
       status code n, group n
 = = DEFINITION RESPONSIBILITY
       position title 1
     ------------------
       position title n
 = = CORPORATE DATA SOURCE
     1. document reference 1 document title 1
     -------------------------------------------
     n. document reference n document title n
 = = STANDARD REPRESENTATION ATTRIBUTES
     JUSTIFICATION                    -   justification
     CODING STRUCTURE                 -   coding structure
     DATA LENGTH                      -   data length
     UNITS OF MEASURE                 -   units of measure
     SCALE FACTOR                     -   scale factor
     NUMERIC TYPE                     -   numeric type
     NUMERIC PRECISION                -   numeric precision
     NUMERIC VALUE                    -   numeric value
     STORAGE FORMAT                   -   storage format
     RECORDING MODE                   -   recording mode
     STORAGE LENGTH                   -   storage length
 = = ACCESS AUTHORITY
       access authority 1
     --------------------
       access authority n
 = = AUTHORIZED USERS
       authorized user 1 (access options 1)
     ----------------------------------------
       authorized user n (access options n)
 = = VALUE SET ASSIGNMENT RESPONSIBILITY
       value set assignment group 1
     ------------------------------
       value set assignment group n
 = = ENTITY CLASS MEMBERSHIP
       entity class name
```

Figure 3.3 Contents of an attribute definition

```
= = GROUP MEMBERSHIP
      logical group name 1
      ─────────────────────────
      logical group name n
= = IMS SEGMENT MEMBERSHIP
      physical segment name 1
      ─────────────────────────
      physical segment name n
= = RECORD MEMBERSHIP
      logical record name 1
      ─────────────────────────
      logical record name n
= = INTERACTIONS
      interaction 1 library entry name 1
      ──────────────────────────────────
      interaction n library entry name n
= = VALIDITY/EDIT RULES
      1. edit rule 1
      ───────────────
      n. edit rule n
= = CONSISTENCY
      1. consistency check 1
      ───────────────────────
      n. consistency check n
= = REASONABLENESS
      1. reasonableness rule 1
      ──────────────────────────
      n. reasonableness rule n
= = USAGE PROPAGATION
      1. propagation instruction 1
      ─────────────────────────────
      n. propagation instruction n
= = VALIDATION PROPAGATION
      1. propagation instruction 1
      ─────────────────────────────
      n. propagation instruction n
```

Figure 3.3 (Cont.)

"Description" is a freeform narrative containing a concise definition of the attribute in a form suitable for use in a glossary. It can also be a definitive statement of the values which can be assumed by the attribute and its meaning relative to the organization. This statement can be a description of the formats used in specific representation.

"Attribute function" is a freeform narrative describing the purpose and usage of the attribute as it relates to corporate objectives and the business functions used to achieve them.

"Definition update source" is a composite structure identifying the individuals or groups who updated the entry in the dictionary and the dates on which those updates were made.

"User acceptance status" is a composite structure identifying the project teams or organizational groups who created the definition or who must be informed of its subsequent updates. The status code is a 1-character code representing the degree of acceptance of the entry in the dictionary relative to the group identified by "group norm." For example, code A may mean that the definition in its current form has been accepted as a working definition by the associated group. Changes in the definition can only be made after consultation with that group.

"Definition responsibility" is a set of references to the organizational groups charged with the responsibility for the accuracy and ongoing integrity of a definition.

"Corporate data source" is a set of references to corporate documentation which can be considered a definitive reference source for the coding schemas associated with an attribute. For example, the source for the definition may be a corporate general circular—G.C. 206-9-01, "Management Salary Administration Policies and Procedures."

The entries for "standard representation attributes" are self-explanatory. Therefore, I will give an example without any definitions, as follows:

```
JUSTIFICATION        —   LEFT
CODING STRUCTURE     —   ALPHABETIC
DATA LENGTH          —   30 CHARACTERS
UNITS OF MEASURE     —   KILOMETERS
SCALE FACTOR         —   1000
NUMERIC TYPE         —   INTEGER
NUMERIC PRECISION    —   5 DIGITS
NUMERIC VALUE        —   POSITIVE
STORAGE FORMAT       —   BINARY
RECORDING MODE       —   FIXED
STORAGE LENGTH       —   2 BYTES
```

"Access authority" is a set of references to the organizational groups who have the right to grant access to attribute values.

"Authorized users" is a set of references to the organizational groups who have been granted access privileges to the information represented by the attribute. The access options identify a specific access option granted by the authorized user. For example, an access option R would indicate that the user has read-only access to the attribute values.

"Value set assignment responsibility" is a set of references to the organizational groups who have the right to add to, delete from, or otherwise modify the set of acceptable values which can be assumed by attributes.

"Entity class membership" is a reference to the entity class which includes the attribute as a component.

"Logical group membership," "IMS segment membership," and "logical record membership" are essentially a list of names identifying the group which contains the physical representation of the attribute.

"Interactions" is a collection of references to other entries in the data dictionary reflecting specific relationships between the definitions. The code "interaction" can be a target entity, while "library entry name" identifies an entity class definition describing the entity class for which the attribute is a symbolic reference pointer.

"Validity-edit rules" is a freeform narrative listing the edit rules which must be satisfied by attribute values stored in groups, segments, or similar physical data structures.

"Consistency checks" is a freeform narrative listing the consistency checks which must be satisfied by all attribute values. For example, the attribute value for the attribute "month" cannot be greater than 12.

"Reasonableness" checks is a narrative listing the reasonableness checks which, when applied against attribute values, identify values which are unreasonable and should be further investigated.

"Usage propagation" is a freeform narrative describing the impact of changes made to attribute values held in physical data structures and the steps which must be taken to propagate the changes throughout the database. The narrative may include a list of the names of other attributes affected by the changes.

"Validation propagation" is a freeform narrative describing the impact of changes to the set of acceptable values which can be assumed by an attribute, and the actions necessary to update the acceptable values of other related attributes. This entry is used as part of the database integrity controls to ensure that changes in the set of acceptable attribute values are propagated to other related attributes whose value sets are also affected.

Examples of entries in the attribute volume of the data dictionary and retrieval of the entries will be given in later chapters.

Finally, Appendixes A to D give detailed coverage of entries for "entity class," "logical group," "IMS database," and "logical schema" definitions.

3.6 Application of the Data Dictionary

The data dictionary defined in previous sections can be used either actively or passively. It can be used to store definitive information about data and processes. It provides information about the meaning of data entities as they are used. It provides information on the physical attributes and placement of data entities and relationships.

The data dictionary can be used in an active mode to cluster the attribute into entity classes, the entity classes into an entity model, and the entity model into a logical schema from which the physical databases are built.

The data dictionary can be used as a documentation tool. It can also be used to check the accuracy of the existing documentation. It can be a powerful tool used by internal auditors to audit and monitor application systems, access to stored data, and access violations.

The data dictionary described here can be tailored to actively interface with the organization's computer operating system to deny access to unauthorized users.

In a passive mode the data dictionary can be used to identify and notify affected users of changes made in existing data definitions. In an active mode it can determine the users of shared data and control the use of that shared resource.

The data dictionary can be used to facilitate data integration and reduce redundancy in the storage of data. Finally, the data dictionary can interface with the operating system to produce access statistics which will enable the database administrators to tune and reorganize the database.

3.7 Examples of Use of an In-House Data Dictionary

The data dictionary being defined here is currently being used for data analysis, documentation, and as an aid in physical design.

The following section will demonstrate current usages of the data dictionary and enable the reader to cluster attributes into entities and entities into their logical schemas.

In Figures 3.4 to 3.6 it is shown that the attribute "building or administrative unit" is part of the entity class "building" which in turn is part of the "building logical schema." The logical group illustrated in Figure 3.5 is a set of attributes grouped together on the basis of common usage, access requirements, or source. For example, the logical group "address" will comprise the attributes "street," "city," "state," and "country."

In tracing the attribute from the data dictionary entry to the physical database, one would obtain the attribute "name," then find it under the attribute heading "entity class" or the contents heading "logical group," and follow it to the "logical schema membership" and the "IMS database representation" headings of the "logical schema" definition.

3.8 Retrieval from the Data Dictionary

Access to the data dictionary is provided by a set of application programs written in Mark IV and run under the IBM Time Sharing Option (TSO).

```
= = NAME: BUILDING/ADMIN. UNIT RELATIONSHIP POINTER
= = DESCRIPTION
    This is the symbolic pointer from the building to the
    associated plant unit. It consists of a valid ADMINISTRATIVE
    UNIT CODE.

= = FUNCTION
    To set the relationship between a building and all the
    associated ADMINISTRATIVE UNITS and to provide direct access
    to ADMINISTRATIVE UNIT CODES via the BUILDING CODE.

= = GROUP MEMBERSHIP
    Building and administrative unit relationship group

= = ENTITY CLASS MEMBERSHIP
    Building

= = INTERACTIONS
    Element type, common language location
    Identification code
    Target entity—administrative unit

= = CLASSIFICATION
    Attribute definition

= = USER ACCEPTANCE STATUS
    P, CLLI

= = DEFINITION RESPONSIBILITY
    Section supervisor—common language and coding systems

= = VALUE SET ASSIGNMENT RESPONSIBILITY
    Section supervisor—common language and coding systems
```

Figure 3.4   Attribute definition

```
= = NAME: BUILDING/ADMIN. UNIT RELATIONSHIP GROUP
= = DESCRIPTION
    This group identifies a relationship between a BUILDING and
    an ADMINISTRATIVE UNIT. The group constitutes one part of a
    bidirectional relationship. The group is composed of a
    symbolic pointer to an ADMINISTRATIVE UNIT which is
    associated with the BUILDING.

= = CLASSIFICATION
    Logical group (relationship)

= = LOGICAL SCHEMA MEMBERSHIP
    Building

= = USER ACCEPTANCE STATUS
    P, CLLI

= = CONTENTS
    Building and administrative unit relationship group
    Building and administrative unit relationship pointer
```

Figure 3.5   Logical group definition

```
= = NAME: BUILDING
= = DESCRIPTION
    A building is any existing or proposed structure or part of
    a structure which normally contains telephone company
    equipment or personnel. This includes central office
    buildings, business and commercial office buildings,
    customer buildings, independent telephone company buildings,
    building complex areas within a structure, and other similar
    structures.

= = FUNCTION
    Used to record the street address, land location, and
    construct type of structures.

= = CLASSIFICATION
    Entity class

= = USER ACCEPTANCE STATUS
    P, CLLI

= = ATTRIBUTES
    Building code
    Building designation
    Building ownership status
    Building construction type
    Building street address
    Building and administrative relationship pointer
    Building and traffic unit relationship pointer
    Building and plant unit relationship pointer
```

Figure 3.6 Entity class definition

These programs were developed in-house as part of the research on data dictionaries.

There are four major deliverables from these programs:

- *Glossary.* A 4-line abstract from the description heading of any entity in the dictionary.

- *Index.* A complete output of all entries in the data dictionary.

- *Relationship.* A linkage of attribute to logical group, to entity class, to logical schema, and finally to physical database.

- *Hardcopy.* A printed listing of complete definitions or complete dictionary contents, or a partial listing by the various headings, e.g., "description" and "classification."

3.9 Practical Uses of In-House Data Dictionaries

In a major survey which I conducted in 1983 to determine (1) the use of data dictionaries, (2) the adequacy and effectiveness of current manufacturer's data dictionaries, and (3) the move to develop in-house

CAMROSE LUTHERAN COLLEGE
LIBRARY

dictionaries, it was established that the major dissatisfaction with current data dictionaries was their inability to model the business activities of the corporation.

Today, major corporations are interested in developing entity models of their business activities. Information systems planning (ISP) and business systems planning (BSP) are two activities which occupy the time of business analysts. These activities seek to develop models which translate the objectives and goals of the corporation into business systems.

For example, the executives of company A may have as their stated goal "to increase our share of the automobile market by 50 percent." The business analyst determines (1) the entities required to satisfy this objective and (2) the relationships among those entities.

The current dictionaries have no facilities to include definitive information about these objectives, entities, and relationships. The in-house data dictionary described in earlier sections of this chapter comes closest to being able to include such information. This dictionary can define the processes and systems, entity model, logical schemas, and physical databases needed to produce information to satisfy the user's requirements.

3.10 Summary

This chapter detailed an in-house data dictionary developed during a 3-year period of research. The dictionary contained nine elements, as follows:

- Attribute
- Entity class
- Element
- Logical group
- Logical schemas
- Logical records
- Logical files
- IMS databases
- IMS segments

Definitive information was given about the entries in each element. Some of these entries are "function," "description," "classification," and "validity-edit rules." Examples were given which showed how an attribute could be traced to an entity class, to a logical schema, and then to the IMS database.

The method for retrieving data from the dictionary was described, and examples of the retrieval data were given. Some of this data included:

- *Glossary.* A 4-line abstract from the description heading of any entity in the dictionary.
- *Index.* Complete output of all entries in the data dictionary.
- *Relationship.* Linkage of attribute to logical group, to entity class, to logical schema, and finally to physical database.
- *Hardcopy.* A printed listing of complete definitions or complete dictionary contents, or a partial listing by various headings, e.g., "description" and "classification."

The chapter ended with a detailed description of the uses of this in-house data dictionary and showed how the dictionary can be used to develop systems to meet the requirements of corporate users.

4

A Method for Entering Data into the Data Dictionary

Introduction

This chapter describes a method used to enter data into the various sections of the data dictionary discussed in Chapter 3.

The method described here assumes that the user's facility operates computer equipment that can utilize the IBM software packages: Multiple Virtual Systems (MVS), Time Sharing Option (TSO), and Document Composition Facility (DCF).

4.1 Data Entry

The user who intends to enter data into any of the dictionary definitions, e.g., attribute, entity class, or logical schema, must define a partitioned data set (PDS) and enter each definition as a member of the PDS.

The convention for using the PDS is as follows:

```
Userid.Volume Identifer.ENTRIES
```

where `Userid` is the user identification number under which the PDS is stored, `Volume Identifer` is a unique 3-letter code which represents the project or system volume, and `Entries` is the software package–naming convention for the PDS.

Each definition must consist of section headings followed by text. For example, the attribute definition will have the headings "Description," "Function," "Classification," "User Acceptance Status," etc., followed by the respective text for each of the headings.

```
EDIT - #20X.PAY.ENTRIES (PAY007) - - - COLS009008
COMMAND INPUT = = =
****** **** TOP OF DATA ************
. . . . . = = NAME
. . . . . = = CLASSIFICATION
. . . . . = = DEFINITION UPDATE SOURCE
. . . . . = = DESCRIPTION
. . . . . = = USER ACCEPTANCE STATUS
. . . . . .
****** *** BOTTOM OF DATA *******
```

Figure 4.1   Section headings in a PDS

4.2   Entering Section Headings

Enter each section heading in capital letters on a new line of the partitioned data-set member. The section heading must be preceded by the delimiter of two equal signs (= =) and starts against the left margin of the member.

Let's assume the headings shown above were entered into member PAY007 of the #20X.PAY.ENTRIES partitioned data set. These section headings would appear in the member as shown in Figure 4.1

4.3   Entering Text Data

The text following the section headings may be in any or all of these forms:

- Paragraphs
- Tables or lists
- Single line
- Combinations of paragraphs and tables

The text may also include the special characters

4.4   Entering Paragraphs

If the text following the section heading is in the form of paragraphs, then the text must be entered left-justified in the partitioned data-set member. The first paragraph may start on the same line as the section heading as long as it is separated from the section heading by a colon (:). Each following paragraph must be justified against the left margin of the member. A blank line separates one paragraph from another paragraph. Figure 4.2 is an example of how to enter paragraphs into the partitioned data-set member. In this example, the first paragraph starts on the same line as the section heading and is separated from the section heading by a colon.

```
EDIT - #20X.PAY.ENTRIES (PAY007) - - - - COLUMNS 0090080
COMMAND INPUT = = =
****** ***** * TOP OF DATA ************
 . . . . . == DESCRIPTION: This is the first section
 . . . . . of the first paragraph of the DESCRIPTION
 . . . . . SECTION.
 . . . . .
 . . . . . This is a new paragraph.
****** **** BOTTOM OF DATA ************
```

Figure 4.2 Paragraphs in a PDS

4.5 Entering Tables or Lists

If the text following the section heading is in the form of tables or lists, the text must be entered on the lines following the section heading. The table can start in any column of the partitioned data-set member.

Figure 4.3 is an example of how to enter tables or lists into the partitioned data-set member.

4.6 Entering Combinations of Paragraphs and Tables

If the text following the section heading is in the form of combinations of paragraphs and tables, the paragraphs data must follow the rules for entering paragraphs. The tabular data must follow the rules for entering tables and lists with the exception that each line must be preceded by at least three blanks.

Figure 4.4 is an example of how to enter combinations of paragraphs and tables into the partitioned data-set member. In this example, the first paragraph starts on the same line as the section heading and is separated from the section heading by a colon. Each table entry is indented 3 spaces.

4.7 Editing Members of a PDS

In order to enter data into a partitioned data set, you edit the data set. If you are using MVS with the SPF facility, to get to the EDIT–ENTRY

```
EDIT - #20X.PAY.ENTRIES (PAY007) - - COLUMNS 009 0080
COMMAND INPUT = = = =
****** **** TOP OF DATA ***************
 . . . . . . == CONTENTS
 . . . . . .      OOAA MEMBER 1
 . . . . . .      OOAA MEMBER 2
****** *** BOTTOM OF DATA ***************
```

Figure 4.3 Tables in a PDS

```
EDIT - #20X.PAY.ENTRIES (PAY007) - - - COLUMNS 009 0080
COMMAND INPUT = =
****** ***** TOP OF DATA ******************
. . . . . = = DESCRIPTION: This is the first sentence
. . . . . . of the first paragraph of the DESCRIPTION section.
. . . . .
. . . . . . TABLE 1
. . . . . . FIRST TABLE LINE
. . . . ..THIS IS THE SECOND PARAGRAPH.
****** ****** BOTTOM OF DATA *********
```

Figure 4.4   Paragraphs and tables in A PDS

PANEL you type in 2 at the SELECT OPTIONS line. The EDIT–ENTRY PANEL will appear as shown in Figure 4.5.

To edit the partitioned data set named #20X.PAY.ENTRIES, type in

1. PROJECT = = = #20X

2. LIBRARY = = = PAY

3. TYPE   = = = ENTRIES

4.8   Editing an Existing Member

To edit a member which already exists and whose name is PAY002, move the cursor beside MEMBER in the EDIT–ENTRY PANEL of Figure 4.5 and type in PAY002. Press the ENTER key, and the member with all the entries should appear.

4.9   Creating a New Member

To create a new member of the PDS, enter the member name in the MEMBER line of Figure 4.5 as follows:

1. PROJECT = = = #20X

2. LIBRARY = = = PAY

```
-------------------------EDIT-ENTRY PANEL -------------------------
ENTER/VERIFY PARAMETERS BELOW
SPF LIBRARY:
  PROJECT = = =
  LIBRARY = = = = = = = = = = = =
  TYPE    = = =
  MEMBER  = = =
  OTHER PARTITIONED OR SEQUENTIAL DATASET:
```

Figure 4.5   The edit-entry panel

3. TYPE   = = = ENTRIES

4. MEMBER   = = = PAY007

Press the ENTER key, and the new member will be created.

4.10   Deleting a Member

To delete a member, get the utility menu and type in SELECT OPTION
= = = 1. The utility menu looks like this:

```
---------------LIBRARY UTILITY --------------
SELECT OPTION = = =
C - COMPRESS DATASET        P - PRINT MEMBER
R - RENAME MEMBER           D - DELETE MEMBER
SPF LIBRARY:
  PROJECT = = =
```

To delete PROJECT #20X, type in SELECT OPTION D and PROJECT
= = = #20X.

4.11   Browsing a PDS

If you want to look at a member without editing it, you may want to
browse the member. To do this, type in

```
SELECT OPTIONS = = = 1
```

Press the ENTER key, and the BROWSE–ENTRY PANEL will appear.

To browse the partitioned data set named #20X.PAY ENTRIES, type
in the material in Figure 4.6.

4.12   Selecting a Member from a PDS

To select a member from a PDS, you must have the BROWSE–ENTRY
PANEL shown in Figure 4.6 on the screen. Go through the steps listed
in section 4.11, leaving the MEMBER = = = line blank, and press the
ENTER key. Then move the cursor to the left of the member you want

```
-------------------------BROWSE-ENTRY PANEL-----------------------
ENTER/VERIFY PARAMETERS BELOW
SPF LIBRARY:
PROJECT = = = #20X
LIBRARY = = = PAY
TYPE    = = = ENTRIES
MEMBER  = = =
```

Figure 4.6   The browse-entry panel

selected and type S. Press the ENTER key, and the member will be selected. The selection will appear as follows:

```
BROWSE - #20X.PAY.ENTRIES ------------
COMMAND INPUT = = =
NAME       VAR.MOD.        CREATED              LAST MODIFIED
PAY002     01.09           86/10/17             86/10/23 10:08
```

4.13   Printing Members from a PDS

The software described in earlier sections of this chapter provides for the following displays of members of PDS's:

- PRINTALL   Print all definitions.
- PRINTSEL   Print selected definitions.
- SELHEADG   Print only the information under selected section headings.
- SELBOTH   Print only the information under selected section headings of selected definitions.
- GLOSSARY   Print the glossary of the definitions.
- RELATION   Print the relationships between definitions.
- BACKUP   Back up the ENTRIES partitioned data set.
- RESTORE   Restore selected members of the entire ENTRIES partitioned data set.

4.14   Examples of a Created
Member of a PDS

The following Data Documentation Index shows examples of a member of a PDS that was created to store data definitions for a tool inventory management system. The examples include

- DOCUMENTATION INDEX
- ATTRIBUTE DEFINITION
- LOGICAL GROUP DEFINITION
- ENTITY CLASS DEFINITION

To use the INDEX, match the reference number (REF) with the number in the center of the first line of each definition. For example, REF00030 matches with the data definition for the attribute SIGNED OUT AGT SERIAL NUMBER.

REF	DESCRIPTION	AUTH
00010	SIGNED OUT TO INSTALLER NAME	JL
00020	SIGNED OUT TO INSTALLER POSITION CODE	JL
00030	SIGNED OUT AGT SERIAL NUMBER	JL
00040	OMEGA PURCHASE NUMBER	JL
00050	ATTACHMENT THIS TOOL IS EQUIPPED WITH	JL
00060	OPTIONAL ATTACHMENT FOR THIS TOOL OR TEST EQUIPMENT	JL
00070	NECESSARY ATTACHMENT OF ANOTHER TOOL	JL
00080	CALIBRATION DATE	JL
00081	REPAIR SHOP	JL
00090	PLANNED RESERVATION INDICATOR	JL
00100	RESERVATION EFFECTIVE DATE	JL
00110	RESERVATION RETURN DATE	JL
00120	DATE AND TIME PLANNED RESERVATION WAS MADE	JL
00130	STORAGE BIN NUMBER	JL
00140	CALIBRATION COST	JL
00150	REPAIR COST	JL
00160	CALIBRATION HOURS	JL
00170	REPAIR HOURS	JL
00180	CALIBRATION SHOP	JL
00190	REPAIR SHOP	JL
00200	CATEGORY OF TOOL	JL
00210	CRITICAL REORDER LEVEL	JL
00220	PURCHASE OR TRANSFER DATE	JL
00230	DATE SIGNED OUT	JL
00240	NAME OF INSTALLER	JL
00250	INSTALLER INITIALS	JL
00260	SIGNED OUT LOCATION	JL
00270	MANUFACTURERS SERIAL NUMBER	JL
00280	TIMES NOT AVAILABLE	JL
00290	SUPPLIER INFORMATION	JL
00300	OMEGA PURCHASE NUMBER	JL
00310	PURCHASE ORDER NUMBER	JL
00320	DESIRED REORDER AMOUNT	JL
00330	INSTALLERS LOCATOR CODE	JL
00340	DATE TOOL IS EXPECTED BACK TO THE TOOL POOL	JL
00350	ACCOUNTING DESCRIPTION	JL
00360	ACCOUNTING DESCRIPTION OF SIMILAR TOOL	JL
00370	NUMBER OF AVAILABLE TOOLS FOR SIGNING OUT	JL
00380	TIMES ONE LEFT	JL
00390	TIMES TWO LEFT	JL
00400	TIMES THREE LEFT	JL
00410	INVENTORY LOCATION OF TOOL	JL
00420	TRADE KEYWORDS USED BY INSTALLERS	JL
00430	QUANTITY OF TOOLS WITH THE SAME ACCOUNTING DESCRIPTION	JL
00440	DAYS TOOL HAS BEEN SIGNED OUT TO INSTALLERS	JL

REF	DESCRIPTION	AUTH
00450	NUMBER OF TIMES TOOL HAS BEEN SIGNED OUT	JL
00460	DATE WRITE OFF WAS MADE	JL
00470	REASON TOOL WAS WRITTEN OFF	JL
00480	WAITLIST RESERVATION INDICATOR	JL
00490	WAITLIST RESERVATION DATE	JL
00500	PURCHASE VALUE	JL
00510	RESERVED BY INSTALLER	JI
00520	WAITLISTED BY INSTALLER	JL
00530	CALIBRATION DATE	JL
00540	AVAILABILITY INDICATOR	JL
00550	LOAN OUT LIMIT	JL
00620	DESCRIPTION OF WHAT TOOL CAN BE USED FOR	JL
00630	ACCOUNTING DESCRIPTION REFERENCE	JL
10010	USAGE STATISTICS	JL
10020	RESERVE INFORMATION	JL
10030	INVENTORY INFORMATION	JL
10040	SUPPLIER - PURCHASE INFORMATION	JL
10060	SIGN IN-OUT INFORMATION	JL
10070	CALIBRATION - REPAIR INFORMATION	JL
10100	TOOL TEXT INFORMATION	JL
10110	TOOLS SIGNED OUT	JL
10120	INDIVIDUAL TOOL ID	JL
10130	TOOL REFERENCES	JL
10140	TOOL GROUP INFORMATION	JL
10150	NAME OF INSTALLER	JL
10160	POSITION CODES	JL
10170	TRADE KEYWORD REFERENCES	JL
30010	TOOL GROUPS	JL
30020	INDIVIDUAL TOOLS	JL
30030	KEYWORDS CATALOGUE TO TOOL GROUPS	JL
30040	INSTALLER POSITION CODE	JL
30050	INSTALLER NAME	JL

DATA DEFINITION   00030   OCT 26 1986   PAGE   1

DATA   00030   JL   OCT 03 1986

LINE   CHAR(AN)   DATA-NAME
020   SIGNED OUT AGT SERIAL NUMBER

        C-E DEC FRMT   ABBREVIATED-DATA-NAME
030   0   S   SIGNED OUT SERIAL

        DATA DESCRIPTION
100   == DESCRIPTION ==
101   A REFERENCE TO A TOOL AGT SERIAL NO THAT IS SIGNED OUT BY
102   AN INSTALLER
103
104   == FUNCTION ==
105   MANAGING THE TOOLS IN THE TOOL POOLS OF EQUIPMENT
106   INSTALLATION
107
108   == CLASSIFICATION ==
109   ATTRIBUTE DEFINITION
110
111   == USER ACCEPTANCE STATUS ==
112   I, NETWORK INFORMATION SYSTEMS
113
114   == DEFINITION RESPONSIBILITY ==
115   MECHANIZATION ANALYST, NETWORK STAFF
116   EQUIPMENT INSTALLATION METHODS SUPERVISOR, NETWORK STAFF
117
118   == CORPORTE DATA SOURCE ==
119   AGX 000-173-005   MANAGEMENT OF MAJOR TOOLS OF TEST
120   NETWORK STAFF   EQUIPMENT ACCOUNT CODE 264-500
121   GENERAL CIRCULAR   OBTAINING AND CONTROLLING TOOLS AND
122   105-15-02   TEST EQUIPMENT
123   GENERAL CIRCULAR   MOTOR VEHICLES, TOOLS AND TEST EQUIPMENT
124   301-2-01
125
126   == STANDARD REPRESENTATION ATTRIBUTES ==
127   POINTER
128
129   == AUTHORIZED USERS ==
130   EQUIPMENT INSTALLATION - NORTH (R, C, D, M)
131   EQUIPMENT INSTALLATION - SOUTH (R, C, D, M)
132   STAFF SUPERVISOR - NETWORK STAFF
133
134   == ACCESS AUTHORITY ==
135   EQUIPMENT INSTALLATION MANAGER - NORTH

```
136        EQUIPMENT INSTALLATION MANAGER - SOUTH
137
138        == VALUE ASSIGNMENT RESPONSIBLITY ==
139        EQUIPMENT INSTALLATION MANAGER - NORTH
140        EQUIPMENT INSTALLATION MANAGER - SOUTH
141        STAFF SUPERVISOR - NETWORK STAFF
142
143        == ENTITY CLASS MEMBERSHIP ==
144        INSTALLER NAME
145
146        == LOGICAL GROUP MEMBERSHIP ==
147        TOOLS SIGNED OUT
148


       RULES/LIMIT-CHECKS/OTHER-EDITS
700        == VALIDITY / EDIT RULES ==
701          MUST BE A VALID AGT SERIAL NO EXISTING IN
702          THE DATA BASE
703
```

DATA DEFINITION   00150   OCT 26 1986   PAGE   1

DATA   00150   JL   AUG 04 1986

LINE   CHAR(AN)   DATA-NAME
020   REPAIR COST

       C-E DEC FRMT   ABBREVIATED-DATA-NAME
030   2   P   REPAIR COST

DATA DESCRIPTION
100   == DESCRIPTION ==
101   THE COST OF REPAIR PERFORMED ON THE TOOL. CAN BE MORE
102   THAN ONE OCCURANCE.
103
104   == AUTHORIZED USERS ==
105   EQUIPMENT INSTALLATION - NORTH (R, C, D, M)
106   EQUIPMENT INSTALLATION - SOUTH (R, C, D, M)
107   STAFF SUPERVISOR - NETWORK STAFF
108
109   == DEFINITION RESPONSIBILITY ==
110   MECHANIZATION ANALYST, NETWORK STAFF
111   EQUIPMENT INSTALLATION METHODS SUPERVISOR, NETWORK STAFF
112
113   == CORPORTE DATA SOURCE ==
114   AGX 000-173-005   MANAGEMENT OF MAJOR TOOLS OF TEST
115   NETWORK STAFF   EQUIPMENT ACCOUNT CODE 264-500
116   GENERAL CIRCULAR   OBTAINING AND CONTROLLING TOOLS AND
117   105-15-02   TEST EQUIPMENT
118   GENERAL CIRCULAR   MOTOR VEHICLES, TOOLS AND TEST EQUIPMENT
119   301-2-01
120
121   == STANDARD REPRESENTATION ATTRIBUTES ==
122   JUSTIFICATION   -   RIGHT
123   CODING STRUCTURE   -   NUMERIC
124   PICTURE   -   9
125   USAGE   -   COMP-3
126   UNITS OF MEASURE   -   DOLLARS
127   SCALE FACTOR   -   1/100
128   RECORDING MODE   -   FIXED
129   STORAGE LENGTH   -   6
130
131   == FUNCTION ==
132   MANAGING THE TOOLS IN THE TOOL POOLS OF EQUIPMENT
133   INSTALLATION
134
135   == AUTHORIZED USERS ==

```
136      EQUIPMENT INSTALLATION - NORTH (R, C, D, M)
137      EQUIPMENT INSTALLATION - SOUTH (R, C, D, M)
138      STAFF SUPERVISOR - NETWORK STAFF
139
140      == DEFINITION RESPONSIBILITY ==
141
142      == ACCESS AUTHORITY ==
143      EQUIPMENT INSTALLATION MANAGER - NORTH
144      EQUIPMENT INSTALLATION MANAGER - SOUTH
145
146      == VALUE ASSIGNMENT RESPONSIBLITY ==
147      EQUIPMENT INSTALLATION MANAGER - NORTH
148      EQUIPMENT INSTALLATION MANAGER - SOUTH
149      STAFF SUPERVISOR - NETWORK STAFF
150
151      == ENTITY CLASS MEMBERSHIP ==
152      INDIVIDUAL TOOL DATA BASE
153
154      == LOGICAL GROUP MEMBERSHIP ==
155      CALIBRATION - REPAIR INFORMATION

         RULES/LIMIT-CHECKS/OTHER-EDITS
700      == VALIDITY / EDIT RULES ==
701      1 TO 999,999,999.99
702
```

```
DATA DEFINITION                00010              OCT 26 1986   PAGE     1
```

DATA   00010   JL   OCT 05 1986

LINE   CHAR(AN)   DATA-NAME
020   SIGNED OUT TO INSTALLER NAME

        C-E DEC FRMT   ABBREVIATED-DATA-NAME
030   0   S   SIGNED OUT TO

        DATA DESCRIPTION
100   == DESCRIPTION ==
101   A REFERENCE TO THE NAME OF THE INSTALLER THAT
102   HAS THE TOOL SIGNED OUT TO HIM/HER.
103
104   == FUNCTION ==
105   MANAGING THE TOOLS IN THE TOOL POOLS OF EQUIPMENT
106   INSTALLATION
107
108   == CLASSIFICATION ==
109   ATTRIBUTE DEFINITION
110
111   == USER ACCEPTANCE STATUS ==
112   I, NETWORK INFORMATION SYSTEMS
113
114   == DEFINITION RESPONSIBILITY ==
115   MECHANIZATION ANALYST, NETWORK STAFF
116   EQUIPMENT INSTALLATION METHODS SUPERVISOR, NETWORK STAFF
117
118   == CORPORTE DATA SOURCE ==
119   AGX 000-173-005   MANAGEMENT OF MAJOR TOOLS OF TEST
120   NETWORK STAFF   EQUIPMENT ACCOUNT CODE 264-500
121   GENERAL CIRCULAR   OBTAINING AND CONTROLLING TOOLS AND
122   105-15-02   TEST EQUIPMENT
123   GENERAL CIRCULAR   MOTOR VEHICLES, TOOLS AND TEST EQUIPMENT
124   301-2-01
125
126   == STANDARD REPRESENTATION ATTRIBUTES ==
127   POINTER
128
129   == AUTHORIZED USERS ==
130   EQUIPMENT INSTALLATION - NORTH (R, C, D, M)
131   EQUIPMENT INSTALLATION - SOUTH (R, C, D, M)
132   STAFF SUPERVISOR - NETWORK STAFF
133
134   == ENTITY CLASS MEMBERSHIP ==
135   INDIVIDUAL TOOL DATA BASE
```
```

```
136
137        LOGICAL GROUP MEMBERSHIP ==
138        SIGN IN-OUT INFORMATION
139        == ACCESS AUTHORITY ==
140        EQUIPMENT INSTALLATION MANAGER - NORTH
141        EQUIPMENT INSTALLATION MANAGER - SOUTH
142
143        == VALUE ASSIGNMENT RESPONSIBLITY ==
144        EQUIPMENT INSTALLATION MANAGER - NORTH
145        EQUIPMENT INSTALLATION MANAGER - SOUTH
146        STAFF SUPERVISOR - NETWORK STAFF

       RULES/LIMIT-CHECKS/OTHER-EDITS
700        == VALIDITY / EDIT RULES ==
701            MUST BE AN EMPLOYEE EXISTING IN THE PPA DATA BASE
702
```

DATA DEFINITION   00040   OCT 26 1986   PAGE   1

DATA   00040   JL   OCT 05 1986

LINE   CHAR(AN)   DATA-NAME
020   TOOL AND TEST EQUIPMENT AGT SERIAL NUMBER

        C-E DEC FRMT   ABBREVIATED-DATA-NAME
030   0   C   AGT SERIAL

        DATA DESCRIPTION
100   == DESCRIPTION ==
101   THE NUMBER USED BY OMEGA SYSTEM FOR THIS KIND OF TOOL
102   EACH INDIVIDUAL TOOL IS IDENTIFIED BY THE ENGRAVED AGT SERIAL
103
104   #, WHERE EACH NUMBER IS UNIQUE.
105
106
107   == FUNCTION ==
108   MANAGING THE TOOLS IN THE TOOL POOLS
109   INSTALLATION
110
111   == CLASSIFICATION ==
112   ATTRIBUTE DEFINITION
113
114   == USER ACCEPTANCE STATUS ==
115   I, NETWORK INFORMATION SYSTEMS
116
117   == DEFINITION RESPONSIBILITY ==
118   MECHANIZATION ANALYST, NETWORK STAFF
119   EQUIPMENT INSTALLATION METHODS SUPERVISOR, NETWORK STAFF
120
121   == CORPORTE DATA SOURCE ==
122   AGX 000-173-005   MANAGEMENT OF MAJOR TOOLS OF TEST
123   NETWORK STAFF   EQUIPMENT ACCOUNT CODE 264-500
124   GENERAL CIRCULAR   OBTAINING AND CONTROLLING TOOLS AND
125   105-15-02   TEST EQUIPMENT
126   GENERAL CIRCULAR   MOTOR VEHICLES, TOOLS AND TEST EQUIPMENT
127   301-2-01
128   GENERAL CIRCULAR   MOTOR VEHICLES, TOOLS AND TEST EQUIPMENT
129
130   == STANDARD REPRESENTATION ATTRIBUTES ==
131   CODING STRUCTURE   - ALPHANUMERIC
132   JUSTIFICATION   - LEFT
133   PICTURE   - X
134   CODING STRUCTURE   - ALPHANUMERIC
135   USAGE   - DISPLAY

DATA DEFINITION   00040   OCT 26 1986   PAGE   2

```
136
137            UNITS OF MEASURE    -   N/A
138            STORAGE LENGTH      -   7
139
140       == AUTHORIZED USERS ==
141       EQUIPMENT INSTALLATION - NORTH (R, C, D, M)
142       EQUIPMENT INSTALLATION - SOUTH (R, C, D, M)
143       STAFF SUPERVISOR - NETWORK STAFF
144
145       == ACCESS AUTHORITY ==
146       EQUIPMENT INSTALLATION - NORTH (R, C, D, M)
147       EQUIPMENT INSTALLATION - SOUTH (R, C, D, M)
148       STAFF SUPERVISOR - NETWORK STAFF
149
150       == VALUE ASSIGNMENT RESPONSIBLITY ==
151       EQUIPMENT INSTALLATION MANAGER - NORTH
152       EQUIPMENT INSTALLATION MANAGER - SOUTH
153       STAFF SUPERVISOR - NETWORK STAFF
154
155
156
157       == LOGICAL GROUP MEMBERSHIP ==
158       INDIVIDUAL TOOL ID

     RULES/LIMIT-CHECKS/OTHER-EDITS
700       == VALIDITY / EDIT RULES ==
701       TWO DIFFERENT TOOLS CAN NOT HAVE THE SAME NUMBER AT
702       THE SAME TIME (A NUMBER CAN NOT BE REUSED UNTIL FIVE
703       YEARS AFTER THE FIRST ONE WITH THAT NUMBER WAS WRITTEN
704       OFF)
705
```

DATA DEFINITION   00020   OCT 26 1986   PAGE   1

DATA   00020   JL   OCT 03 1986

LINE   CHAR(AN)   DATA-NAME
020   SIGNED OUT TO INSTALLER POSITION CODE

        C-E DEC FRMT   ABBREVIATED-DATA-NAME
030   0   S   SIGNED OUT POSITION

        DATA DESCRIPTION
100   == DESCRIPTION ==
101   A REFERENCE TO THE POSITION CODE OF THE INSTALLER THAT
102   HAS THE TOOL SIGNED OUT TO HIM/HER.
103
104   == FUNCTION ==
105   MANAGING THE TOOLS IN THE TOOL POOLS OF EQUIPMENT
106   INSTALLATION
107
108   == CLASSIFICATION ==
109   ATTRIBUTE DEFINITION
110
111   == USER ACCEPTANCE STATUS ==
112   I, NETWORK INFORMATION SYSTEMS
113
114   == DEFINITION RESPONSIBILITY ==
115   MECHANIZATION ANALYST, NETWORK STAFF
116   EQUIPMENT INSTALLATION METHODS SUPERVISOR, NETWORK STAFF
117
118   == CORPORTE DATA SOURCE ==
119   AGX 000-173-005   MANAGEMENT OF MAJOR TOOLS OF TEST
120   NETWORK STAFF   EQUIPMENT ACCOUNT CODE 264-500
121   GENERAL CIRCULAR   OBTAINING AND CONTROLLING TOOLS AND
122   105-15-02   TEST EQUIPMENT
123   GENERAL CIRCULAR   MOTOR VEHICLES, TOOLS AND TEST EQUIPMENT
124   301-2-01
125
126   == STANDARD REPRESENTATION ATTRIBUTES ==
127   POINTER
128
129   == AUTHORIZED USERS ==
130   EQUIPMENT INSTALLATION - NORTH (R, C, D, M)
131   EQUIPMENT INSTALLATION - SOUTH (R, C, D, M)
132   STAFF SUPERVISOR - NETWORK STAFF
133
134   == ENTITY CLASS MEMBERSHIP ==
135   INDIVIDUAL TOOL DATA BASE

DATA DEFINITION	00020	OCT 26 1986 PAGE 2

```
136        == LOGICAL GROUP MEMBERSHIP ==
137        SIGN IN-OUT INFORMATION
138        == ACCESS AUTHORITY ==
139        EQUIPMENT INSTALLATION MANAGER - NORTH
140        EQUIPMENT INSTALLATION MANAGER - SOUTH
141
142        == VALUE ASSIGNMENT RESPONSIBLITY ==
143        EQUIPMENT INSTALLATION MANAGER - NORTH
144        EQUIPMENT INSTALLATION MANAGER - SOUTH
145        STAFF SUPERVISOR - NETWORK STAFF

       RULES/LIMIT-CHECKS/OTHER-EDITS
700        == VALIDITY / EDIT RULES ==
701           MUST BE A VALID POSITION CODE EXISTING IN PPA
702           THE DATA BASE
703
```

DATA DEFINITION   10030   OCT 26 1986   PAGE   1

DATA   10030   JL   OCT 08 1986

LINE   CHAR(AN)   DATA-NAME
020   INVENTORY INFORMATION

        C-E DEC FRMT   ABBREVIATED-DATA-NAME
030   0   INVENTORY INFO

        DATA DESCRIPTION
100   == DESCRIPTION ==
101   CONTAINS ALL INFORMATION THAT IS RELEVANT TO THE
102   INVENTORY DONE ANNUALLY FOR ACCOUNTING DEPT.   THIS
103   INFORMATION IS OF TEXT VALUE ONLY TO THE TOOL POOL.
104
105   == CLASSIFICATION ==
106   LOGICAL GROUP DEFINITION
107
108   == USER ACCEPTANCE STATUS
109   I, NETWORK INFORMATION SYSTEMS
110
111   == DEFINITION RESPONSIBILITY ==
112   SECTION MANAGER, NETWORK INFORMATION SYSTEMS
113   SECTION MANAGER, EQUIPMENT INSTALLATION METHODS
114
115   == CONTENTS ==
116   PURCHASE DATE
117   MANUFACTURERS SERIAL NUMBER
118   PURCHASE ORDER NUMBER
119   WRITE OFF DATE
120   REASON TOOL WAS WRITTEN OFF
121   PURCHASE VALUE
122
123   == REPRESENTATIONS ==
124   ADF - IMSVS.INCLUDE.SOURCE

```
DATA DEFINITION                10040              OCT 26 1986   PAGE    1


DATA   10040   JL       OCT 07 1986

LINE   CHAR(AN)   DATA-NAME
020                SUPPLIER - PURCHASE INFORMATION

       C-E DEC FRMT    ABBREVIATED-DATA-NAME
030        0           SUPPLIER INFO

       DATA DESCRIPTION
100        == DESCRIPTION ==
101        HAS THE INFORMATION RELEVANT TO SUPPLIER OF TOOLS AND
102        THE PURCHASING OF THE TOOLS
103
104        == CLASSIFICATION ==
105        LOGICAL GROUP DEFINITION
106
107        == USER ACCEPTANCE STATUS
108        I, NETWORK INFORMATION SYSTEMS
109
110        == DEFINITION RESPONSIBILITY ==
111        SECTION MANAGER, NETWORK INFORMATION SYSTEMS
112        SECTION MANAGER, EQUIPMENT INSTALLATION METHODS
113
114        == CONTENTS ==
115        CRITICAL REORDER LEVEL
116        SUPPLIER INFORMATION
117        OMEGA PURCHASE NUMBER
118        REORDER AMOUNT
119
120        == REPRESENTATIONS ==
121        ADF - IMSVS.INCLUDE.SOURCE
```

DATA DEFINITION   30010   OCT 26 1986 PAGE   1

DATA   30010   JL   OCT 08 1986

LINE   CHAR(AN)   DATA-NAME
020   TOOL GROUPS

        C-E DEC FRMT   ABBREVIATED-DATA-NAME
030   0   TOOL GROUPS

        DATA DESCRIPTION
100   == DESCRIPTION ==
101   THE DATA BASE CONTAINING THE INFORMATION ABOUT TOOL
102   GROUPS, WHERE EACH TOOL GROUP HAS THE SAME
103   ACCOUNTING DESCRIPTION.   (I.E. THE TOOL INFO COMMON TO
104   ALL TOOLS WITH THE SAME ACCOUNTING DESCRIPTION)
105
106   == USER ACCEPTANCE STATUS ==
107   I, NETWORK INFORMATION SYSTEMS
108
109   == DEFINITION RESPONSIBILITY ==
110   SECTION MANAGER, NETWORK INFORMATION SYSTEMS
111   SECTION MANAGER, EQUIPMENT INSTALLATION METHODS
112
113   == ATTRIBUTES ==
114   OPTIONAL ATTACHMENT FOR THIS TOOL OR TEST EQUIPMENT
115   OPTIONAL ATTACHMENT OF ANOTHER TOOL
116   PLANNED RESERVATION INDICATOR
117   RESERVATION EFFECTIVE DATE
118   RESERVATION RETURN DATE
119   DATE PLANNED RESERVATION WAS MADE
120   STORAGE BIN NUMBER
121   CALIBRATION SHOP
122   REPAIR SHOP
123   CATEGORY OF TOOL
124   CRITICAL REORDER LEVEL
125   TIMES NOT AVAILABLE
126   SUPPLIER INFORMATION
127   OMEGA PURCHASE NUMBER
128   ACCOUNTING DESCRIPTION
129   ACCOUNTING DESCRIPTION OF SIMILAR TOOL
130   NUMBER OF AVAILABLE TOOLS FOR SIGNING OUT
131   TIMES ONE LEFT
132   TIMES TWO LEFT
133   TIMES THREE LEFT
134   INVENTORY LOCATION OF TOOL
135   QUANTITY OF TOOLS WITH THE SAME ACCOUNTING DESCRIPTION

DATA DEFINITION   30010   OCT 26 1986   PAGE   2

```
136        WAITLIST RESERVATION INDICATOR
137        WAITLIST RESERVATION DATE
138        EXEMPT STOCK BIN NUMBER
139        EXEMPT ITEM PURCHASE DATE
140        EXEMPT ITEM NOT AVAILABLE
141        EXEMPT STOCK SUPPLIER INFORMATION
142        EXEMPT ITEM PURCHASE ORDER NO
143        SIMILAR EXEMPT STOCK DESCRIPTION
144        TIMES ONE EXEMPT UNIT LEFT
145        TIMES TWO EXEMPT UNIT LEFT
146        TIMES THRESS EXEMPT UNIT LEFT
147        INVENTORY LOCATION OF EXEMPT STOCK
148        EXEMPT STOCK UNIT MEASURE
149        DESCRIPTION OF WHAT TOOL CAN BE USED FOR
150        RESERVED BY INSTALLER
151        WAITLISTED BY INSTALLER
```

DATA DEFINITION   30020   OCT 26 1986   PAGE   1

DATA   30020   JL   OCT 08 1986

LINE   CHAR(AN)   DATA-NAME
020   INDIVIDUAL TOOLS

        C-E DEC FRMT   ABBREVIATED-DATA-NAME
030   0   INDIVIDUAL TOOLS

        DATA DESCRIPTION
100   == DESCRIPTION ==
101   THE DATA BASE CONTAINING THE INFORMATION ABOUT EACH INDIVIDUAL
102   TOOL HAVING ITS OWN AGT SERIAL NO.
103
104   == FUNCTION ==
105   MANAGING THE TOOLS IN THE TOOL POOLS OF EQUIPMENT INSTALLATION
106
107   == DEFINITION RESPONSIBILITY ==
108   SECTION MANAGER, NETWORK INFORMATION SYSTEMS
109   SECTION MANAGER, EQUIPMENT INSTALLATION METHODS
110
111   == CLASSIFICATION ==
112   ENTITY CLASS DEFINITION
113
114   == ATTRIBUTES ==
115   ATTACHMENT THIS TOOL IS EQUIPPED WITH
116   NECESSARY ATTACHMENT OF ANOTHER TOOL
117   PURCHASE VALUE
118   SIGNED OUT TO INSTALLER NAME
119   SINGED OUT TO INSTALLER CODE
120   TOOL AND TEST EQUIPMENT AGT SERIAL NUMBER
121   CALIBRATION COST
122   REPAIR COST
123   CALIBRATION HOURS
124   REPAIR HOURS
125   PURCHASE OR TRANSFER DATE
126   DATE SIGNED OUT
127   SIGNED OUT LOCATION
128   MANUFACTURERS SERIAL NUMBER
129   PURCHASE ORDER NUMBER
130   DESIRED REORDER AMOUNT
131   DATE TOOL IS EXPECTED BACK TO THE TOOL POOL
132   DAYS TOOL HAS BEEN SIGNED OUT TO INSTALLERS
133   NUMBER OF TIMES TOOL HAS BEEN SIGNED OUT
134   WRITE OFF DATE
135   REASON TOOL WAS WRITTEN OFF

```
DATA DEFINITION                30030              OCT 26 1986    PAGE    1

DATA    30030    JL      OCT 08 1986

LINE    CHAR(AN)    DATA-NAME
020                  KEYWORDS CATALOGUE TO TOOL GROUPS

        C-E DEC FRMT    ABBREVIATED-DATA-NAME
030          0         KEYWORDS

        DATA DESCRIPTION
100         == DESCRIPTION ==
101         THE DATA BASE CONTAINING ALL KEYWORDS REFERENCING TO
102         THE ACCOUNTING DESCRIPTIONS
103
104         == FUNCTION ==
105         MANAGING THE TOOLS IN THE TOOL POOLS OF EQUIPMENT
106         INSTALLATION
107
108         == USER ACCEPTANCE STATUS ==
109         I, NETWORK INFORMATION SYSTEMS
110
111         == DEFINITION RESPONSIBILITY ==
112         SECTION MANAGER, NETWORK INFORMATION SYSTEMS
113         SECTION MANAGER, EQUIPMENT INSTALLATION METHODS
114
115         == CLASSIFICATION ==
116         ENTITY CLASS DEFINITION
117
118         == USER ACCEPTANCE STATUS ==
119         P, NETWORK INFORMATION SYSTEMS
120
121
122         == ATTRIBUTES ==
123         TRADE KEYWORDS USED BY INSTALLERS
124         DATE PLANNED RESERVATION WAS MADE
```

4.15 Summary

This chapter described how to use MVS and TSO to enter data, modify data, and print data from a data dictionary.

It is not my intention to limit the reader to any single piece of software to achieve the above-described functions. The reader can readily use Conversation Monitor System (CMS) under Virtual Memory (VM) to accomplish the same thing. Indeed, any editor available under any operating system can be used.

Use of Data Dictionaries in Online and Distributed Data-Processing Environments

Introduction

Online systems are represented by the following four basic types:

Data inquiry

Data collection

Message switching

File updating

Data inquiry consists of interrogation capabilities without access to actual data files with respect to changing them through any transactions. For example, inventories or account balances may be accessed, as may the status of a reservation request. The *data collection* version extends the inquiry process into a transaction-processing capability, but updating usually takes place in a batch mode at a later time. Input data is not necessarily derived from source documents; however, a source document could be created at that time. Some degree of error-recognition and correction capability is also present, especially if updating does occur at some time after the initial process.

Message switching combines many short and fast communication lines with several longer and slower ones for efficiency in routing and costs involved with high-volume transfers of data. These are typical of reservation systems in which many hundreds or thousands of terminals may be accessing the control computer through long-distance, high-speed lines while nearby installations use a few low-speed lines, all controlled by a switching process before they actually enter the CPU.

In a *file-updating application* the entire process of inquiry, collection, and updating can take in a totally real-time mode which presents obvious control considerations.

The control issues which are inherent in such advance systems are categorized into the following set of basic types:

Unauthorized access

Data-file controls

Transmission-line controls

Audit-trail considerations

Output controls

Failure and recovery consideration

5.1   Unauthorized Access

Prevention of unauthorized access to the various stages of the online, real-time system is critical to the overall security and accuracy of operations.

The controls against unauthorized access fall into two categories: physical and logical.

Physical controls are measures taken to prevent entry or access to installations. The standard safeguards needed in most installations will be security guards, locks and keys, and personal identification.

Logical controls are measures taken to prevent access to the stored data. These include

Password or terminal identification

Verification routines

Audit or management control logs

Recording of unsuccessful attempts at terminal or data-file access

Separate identification or authorization procedures can be installed to limit the access to certain programs or files as well as to prevent unauthorized writing or altering of files or data records. Again, these attempts can be recorded in a control log to determine

Who is using the system?

What processes are being requested and performed?

What results have been obtained?

What was the time and date of these requests?

To ensure that these logical controls are effectively utilized, a monitoring or review function should also be in existence. A cyclical review of the proper procedures performed each day is usually sufficient and should include the proper sign-on and sign-off procedures, unsuccessful attempts, and attempts to override or patch controls and programs during operations. A procedure known as "real-time notification" can be used to alert the auditors to predetermined limits or processes that have been violated. This method automatically initiates reports to the auditor for reference to a control group for investigation on a relatively timely basis since initiating transaction creates the report immediately after being entered.

5.2 Loss of Audit Trail

While the real-time system offers the benefits of great speed without the usual collection of documentation, new implications arise for the auditors as well. In many cases no source document or intermediate paper trail will exist that would enable the auditor to physically follow a particular transaction from beginning to end, as would be possible in most other systems. Since management will also be interested in maintaining the same type of transaction trail, it is highly recommended that such provisions be incorporated into the initial design and implementation stages of the online real-time application.

One of the problems directly associated with such advanced systems is the lack of what would normally be considered adequate separation of duties by organizational personnel. With more internally generated types of transactions and a system in which backup methods may not be maintained for more than a short time, some form of historical documentation is necessary to provide management and auditors with documentation of what has been happening. One of the most frequently used methods of accomplishing this task is through the creation of a history log. This type of control can identify the time and date as well as the text of the particular transaction. Some versions of this control feature also capture the before and after status of the record file being used as an additional recovery option in the event of a system failure.

Other possible solutions to the lack of a clear audit trail are periodic dumps of the processing file, which may then be stored safely elsewhere, and printer devices installed at the input terminals to create a source of document where none existed before.

5.3   Transmission Errors and Controls

In most instances a real-time system is used because a large number of remote locations will be accessing the central processor. The data is usually transmitted over communications networks that must be protected from errors and penetration. The first important consideration with such a transmission procedure is the correct matching of the system's needs with the particular type of communications chosen to send the data. Some types of networks may also be more susceptible to penetration or interceptions which the organization does not know about.

Two well-known kinds of message interception or manipulation are wiretapping and radiation capture. An outside terminal or other device may be employed to tap a line of communication in order to receive or send messages. For transmissions that are susceptible to interception, it may be necessary to locate terminals which might emit such signals away from exterior walls to reduce the possibility of an outsider being able to record and later decipher these signals. This type of problem may be reduced by use of encryption techniques. Either a block cipher or a stream cipher can be used to code messages in which a substitution code transforms the messages into unintelligible form.

To ensure that messages are sent and received correctly, various error-detection procedures are available. Certain error-detection codes can identify errors as they occur, through various types of control totals which may be programmed to require a retransmission or reverse transmission for verification. Time and date coding may be a part of each message, and usually each transmission is assigned a sequence number which can highlight delayed or missing records.

In addition, each message could contain a beginning and an ending label, as well as an end-of-transmission label for larger groups of messages. A history log can be employed to record all valid and invalid messages for future analysis or emergency recovery capability. In all cases, a control program or terminal should have software monitoring control over the transmission functions to detect problems or failures.

5.4   Data-File Controls

As the transaction process continues from data entry to transmission, the next area of concern is data-file protection and controls. The relationship between transactions and programs is reversed in real-time application in that it is the transaction that uses a particular program or programs, in contrast to batch systems, in which the converse occurs. In addition, multiple users may need a particular data file at or near the same time, which could lead to two possible problems: (1) conflicts over priorities and (2) errors caused by incomplete or inaccurate updating. A supervisory program is usually employed to prevent application programs from getting directly at the database. This exclusive control function is responsible for granting permission for such access. While one program is using a file, others are prevented or locked out until control is passed back to the supervisory routine. This control eliminates the possibility of a deadlock which otherwise might occur, say when two programs are using two different files, each of which is concurrently needed by the other program.

To prevent errors and loss of data records, various techniques are used to protect the integrity of the database. As described earlier, dual recording of transactions and the before and after versions of data records can be used to reconstruct damaged records or errors produced during destructive updating.

5.5 Output Controls

Techniques of audit and control in relation to the output of a real-time system vary with respect to the quantity and security of the data involved. If inquiry requests are involved, the main concern will be to ensure the correct transfer of the data and the verification of the user's authority. If a large quantity of transacted output is present, the control concerns will be more complex and will include accuracy or reasonableness checks as well. Special programs can be used to verify that the originating transactions were received and processed without abnormal indicators of accuracy or completeness.

Output logs are sometimes used to record the information created and can be very useful for statistical comparisons and audit trail considerations.

A system of closed-loop verification may be used in which a positive confirmation of the receipt of data transmitted for processing is returned to the sender. This system can also be helpful in auditing procedures. In case the system or some peripheral device should fail, provisions should be made in the software for a supervisory program function to automatically reroute or retransmit affected output data.

5.6 Evaluation of Controls

In the online, real-time computer system, a proper evaluation of controls which should be in place as well as those which are in operation is necessary as a basis for any reliance on their use in system testing.

Proper documentation is one important element required for auditors to understand how and why the system operates as it does. With the loss of many conventional audit procedures inherent in such advanced systems, adequate description of the steps and stages of processing and record keeping will be the basis for choosing how the subsequent compliance and substantive testing will be done. In most other situations where technical competence may be imperfect, the auditors should consider enlisting the assistance of audit specialists who possess the necessary expertise in online, real-time systems.

The compliance testing procedures of the audit must be extended to include all processes of the system that can affect its accuracy and integrity. The security measures of the organization, the recovery procedures for processing, and the system maintenance all must be afforded careful consideration. In addition, the procedures for file balancing and system testing will be important considerations for the auditor. The substantive testing procedures should include general as well as specific audit software routine.

5.7 The Distributed Data-Processing Environment

Distributed data processing (DDP) can be defined as the functional distribution and cooperative processing of applications among multiple computing nodes interconnected by a communications network for information transfer.

The concept of applications is very general. In a distributed computing system, processing at a computing node is accomplished by users with terminals, executive services activated by executive control language, system software modules activated by the command language, and application programs. The processing is controlled by one or more executive software systems located at various nodes.

The definition of a distributed system includes communication as a necessary but not sufficient condition. An important and mandatory characteristic of distributed systems is multiple control locations. There must, in addition, be processing and data-storage capabilities at the remote geographic locations. The processing and storage elements at the various locations may be the same size and may have the same size compatibility and functionality or may differ in all these factors. For example, an intelligent terminal at one location attached to a host mainframe at another location would qualify as a distributed system.

In addition to communication as a necessary condition, different geographic locations are also a necessary condition for a distributed system. This rules out the kinds of systems termed "loosely coupled," including systems which are limited to front-end communication processors, back-end database processors, data-entry processors, spooling processors, separate I/O processors, maintenance processors, or shared mass-storage systems at a single location. Although any of these processing approaches may be present in a distributed system, they are neither necessary nor significant. Two different terms have been applied to distributed systems in the literature. A *distributed processing system* is defined as a system with processing capability and software dispersed throughout a number of sites linked by real-time communications, but with a centralized database. Peripherals may or may not be distributed. In contrast, a *distributed database system* has portions of the database dispersed throughout a number of sites linked by real-time communications, and with sufficient processing power at each site to manipulate the database.

Because the term "distributed system" is not rigorous, it is instructive to identify system configurations that are excluded from the class of distributed systems. The definition excludes a system composed of a single mainframe, even though some modern computers have been characterized as distributed because they had separate I/O sections or channels.

As mentioned earlier, communications alone do not qualify a system as distributed. Likewise, a front-end processor that controls communication does not qualify as distributed, because it is dedicated to a single function and does not execute applications. The same requirement for nodes to execute application software excludes a single host with a collection of remote terminals even if they do some editing and formatting. Thus, some intelligent terminal systems are excluded.

A *distributed computer system* is composed of a number of elements and has two or more nodes. A node is a complete computer system at a single location. The term "system" will be used to refer to the set of all communicating nodes. A *node* consists of a processing and storage complex called the "host," along with a communications port, including hardware and software. The host may range in size from a large multiprocessor down to a microprocessor, and also includes the associated operating-system software and application programs. A *terminal* is a human interface to the host or to a communications port. *Transmission links* transfer data between communication ports. A *path* is a series of end-to-end links that establishes a data route across part of the distributed system.

5.8 Replication and Partition in a DDP Environment

When data is replicated, two or more copies of the same data exist in the system, and as an extreme, every node could have its own copy of some data. The benefits of replicating data are substantial improvements in performance, cost, tunability, and reliability. There are no misses with a replicated database. However, these benefits come at the cost of greatly complicated update to retain consistency in the several copies of the data. Performance is a critical issue in the use of replicated data, because several of the algorithms used to maintain data consistency require extensive communication among nodes to avoid long delays in update.

Achieving optimum performance in distributed data systems is a complex problem depending on miss rates, update frequency, number of nodes, data distribution method, amount of data, and communication speed and cost.

The most appropriate method of distributing small amounts of data is to simply replicate, especially if the real-time update frequency is low, because the additional storage cost is low. When the updates scan, they are sent to all locations holding a copy, using one of the synchronization algorithms available. This approach is especially attractive when updates are batched and high query performance and reliability are important.

When data is partitioned, the total data is divided into disjointed sets, with one set assigned to each node. Only one copy of each record or data item exists, and it is assigned to some node as its home location at any instant of time. Usually the objective is to assign data to the node most frequently accessing it, to minimize response time and communications. However, not all accesses at a node can be satisfied by data at that node, so the system data directory must be used to transfer the access to the proper location. Accesses that cannot be handled locally are called "exceptions," or "misses." If the application characteristics are such that the data can be partitioned to make all accesses local, this represents an extreme case of partitioning and the data is said to be segmented into completely disjointed sets.

5.9 Data Dictionary and Directories for DDP

Just as data can be partitioned or replicated, or made redundant by using some combination of these procedures, so can the system data dictionary or directory be partitioned or replicated, or distributed in some combination of these procedures. In addition, the directory may be centralized.

The choice among these alternatives must depend on the same considerations as distributing the data, although there is no reason to assume that for a given system the application characteristics of the directory will be similar to the data it points to. For example, in one system the data might have a high update frequency but the directory might have a low update frequency. Conversely, in another system the opposite might be true, for example, in a system with partitioned data and dynamic relocation of data based on usage. Generally, directories exhibit the characteristics of high access rate, low update rate, and high reliability requirements. This is often best met by using a replicated directory.

In a literal sense, directories can be treated the same as data, with one critical difference: the location information for the directory itself must be known to the system nodes in an a priori manner. This can be accomplished by storing the locations of the directory at every node; since they are moved seldom or never, certainly they are retrieval-intensive.

Treating the directory as ordinary data has another advantage. The normal system functions, such as storage management, recovery, security, and update synchronization, automatically become available for the directories.

5.10   Using a Schema to Describe DDP Data

A schema is a description of data formats and relationships among data elements. In distributed systems the concept of storage schema is broadened into a global schema and a local schema. The concept of storage schema is likewise broadened into a global storage schema and a local storage schema. The concept of user schema is extended from a single node to multiple nodes. This broadening and extension is shown diagrammatically in Figure 5.1.

A global schema reflects the logical unity of the entire distributed database. It describes all the data in the system, including formats and relationships, without regard for the actual location of the data. It defines which portions of the data are partitioned, which are replicated, and which are centralized. It defines recovery and synchronization techniques. If the software approach is one of early binding, the information in the global schema is reflected in the code generated from the various nodes. If the system uses late binding, the global schema may be referenced on every access. As such, the global schema, like any other kind of system data, may be replicated, partitioned, or centralized. In general, early binding provides high performance by

```
CENTRALIZED              DISTRIBUTED
                         GLOBAL SCHEMA
SCHEMA                   LOCAL SCHEMA
USER SCHEMA              USER SCHEMA
                         GLOBAL STORAGE SCHEMA
STORAGE SCHEMA           LOCAL STORAGE SCHEMA
```

Figure 5.1 Extension of schema constructs

generating code reflecting the definition and relation of data items, while late binding provides greater flexibility because the schema is interrogated on every access, but performance is lower.

The storage schema must also be generalized. The global storage schema defines the allocation of data to nodes. In the case of replicated data, it defines what nodes have copies. In the case of partitioned data, it defines what nodes have what partitions. The function of allocation of data to specific devices of a node, formerly called the "storage schema," must now be handled by a local storage schema.

The user's view of the data—the "user schema"—also requires extension in meaning. A particular user schema may refer to all data in the system, only to data at a single node, or to parts of data structure spread across several nodes.

Whereas the global schema defines the logical format and relationship for the system without regard to location, the local schema defines the logical formats and relationships as a specific node. For data which is purely local, and for which there is no outside access, the local schema is the only logical definition in existence. For data which may be accessed from the outside, the local schema is a subset of the global schema.

5.11 Dynamic Distribution of Data

Although partitioned data in the DDP system may actually be static in its allocation to nodes, the individual data items may move from node to node, generally based on usage frequency patterns.

Directories also can be distributed on either a static or a dynamic basis. A directory could initially be centralized. Based on access patterns, partitions of the database could be distributed to nodes accessing it frequently.

Dynamic distribution of data offers the potential benefit of reducing exception references, because available storage at an individual node can be used more efficiently. Statistics on data usage must be kept . Data must be periodically relocated and the appropriate directories updated with locks.

Dynamic data distribution is analogous to, but more complex than, online reorganization of centralized databases. Dynamic data reorganization is rarely used in centralized databases because of its complexity. Instead, the database is periodically withdrawn from service, reorganized, and placed in service again. A similar procedure can be used in a distributed database if the application allows it to be temporarily withdrawn from service.

The instrumentation data are still required to develop frequency of use, and directories are still updated. However, most of the benefits of a dynamic database can be obtained even though the database is distributed statically between updates.

Compromises are available between these two extremes of static and dynamic, using, for example, reorganized copies of databases with concurrent updates of both copies. One scheme described in the literature draws on both static and dynamic strategies to minimize operational cost of transaction management.

5.12   Transaction Management

Two general approaches to transaction management can be identified for nonlocal transactions for partitioned databases:

- Transactions sent to data at an alien node and the response returned
- Alien data sent to transactions at the local node

The first of these approaches, using static data, can be best visualized in the case of a single query to a database. An example of this could be an access to a credit reference for a customer whose account is at a remote location.

There are several advantages to the approach of routing transactions to data. Cooperative processing among incompatible systems is simplified because the transaction command is at a high level, is independent of node characteristics, and can be interpreted in a local context. If the transaction must process considerable data or make several accesses, the transmission of the transaction involves much less communication then sending the data. Security and recovery can also be easier to administer, because the transaction, once transmitted, becomes the same as a local transaction. Multiple copies of data are avoided, and considerable processing is done at the alien node.

In this credit-verification example, the query was satisfied by data at a single node. This is the simplest case to be considered, and it is also a very common situation in actual applications. The next order of complexity occurs when the data required exists at several nodes, but the transaction can be partitioned such that each transaction statement accesses, at most, one alien node. This partitionable transaction can still be handled by a static data procedure. The several accesses can in principle be done in parallel, thus improving performance. However, deadlock becomes much more difficult to handle in this case.

The principal benefit in the static-data case is that the data is always accessed at its local node.

If partitioning the transaction is not possible, it may be necessary to employ a static-transaction procedure. Low-level accesses are sent to the appropriate alien nodes, and the data is brought to the local node. The use of a low-level access means that the processing cannot be done at the alien node, and much more data must be sent to the local node. The low-level access means that a much higher level of internode compatibility must exist, to the extent of requiring a common data model.

A common data model requires commonality of data structures, data description, data-manipulation procedures, security access lists, and consistency constraints.

In this static-transaction approach, processing is always done at the originating node, and partitionability of the transaction is not required. Data required for processing is brought to the local node. This causes a risk that large amounts of data may be communicated, but processing power is limited to the requesting nodes. Thus, pure database nodes with no terminals need very little processing power. If data is to be used several times at the requesting node, the node can act as a local cache to avoid the necessity for reacquiring the data.

A system with the combination of static transactions and dynamic distribution of data is referred to as a "data exchange system." Transactions are static, and active data is stored at the node most recently requesting it. A complete copy of the data is stored at a central database. This makes for more efficient use of storage at nodes because only active data is stored; it also makes for efficient use of communication because data is stored where it is used.

Clearly, the choice between a static-data approach and a static-transaction approach is heavily application-dependent. If a large number of transactions are to be performed on a small amount of data, the static-transaction procedure is preferred. If large amounts of data are involved, and the transaction is partitionable, the static-data procedure is preferred.

5.13   The Role of the Data Dictionary in Defining the DDP System

The data dictionary plays a very important role in defining the various components and aspects of the DDP system. In this section I will discuss how the dictionary is used to define the various aspects of the following components:

- Data
- Applications
- Transactions
- Security controls
- Geography, including various nodes
- Systems management

- Network configuration
- Database architecture
- User view
- Recovery procedures
- Hardware and software
- Copy libraries

5.14 Data Dictionary Definitions of DDP Data

The criteria for obtaining definitions of DDP data should include a scheme in which the user can easily determine the description, function, database structure, location, and security of the data.

The data dictionary described in previous chapters is well suited for storing metadata about the user data at the various nodes.

Table 5.1 serves to illustrate which definitions in the data dictionary can be used to define various categories of data listed in section 5.13.

5.15 Data to Be Captured for Each Category

The user intent on developing a data dictionary to capture information about the data categories listed in Table 5.1 will want to include the following metadata entries:

Data	Description, function, identification, data characteristics, and node location
Applications	Group identification, data requirements, node where processed, and access requirements
Transactions	Transaction identification, data requirements, access requirements, and node
Security controls	Passwords, equipment identification schemas, user identification numbers, access to data, encoding of transmission, log of access attempts, and encryption
Geography	Node location, data at each node, equipment at each node, and security
Systems management	Setting of goals, allocation of resources, standards and procedures, and planning
Network configuration	Processor, disk storage, line printer, CRT terminals, communicators, and transaction and batch software

TABLE 5.1   Data Categories versus Dictionary Definitions

Data categories	Data dictionary definitions
Data	Attribute, IMS entity Logical schema
Applications	Logical group
Transactions	Logical group
Security controls	Attribute
Geography	Attribute Attribute, entity, logical schema
Systems management	Attribute
Network configuration	Attribute, entity, logical schema
Database architecture	Entity, logical schema
User view	Entity, IMS, logical schema
Recovery procedures	Attribute
Hardware and software	Attribute
Copy libraries	Attribute

Database architecture	Data model and functionality, data definition, data manipulation constructs, and data manipulation commands
User view	Data definition and manipulation, location of data, and security requirements
Recovery procedures	Audit trails, checkpoint rollback procedures, synchronization control procedures, and error-detection procedures.
Hardware and software	List of hardware and software for each node
Copy libraries	Description of source code, data definitions, and standards and procedures that can be moved from node to node

5.16   Summary

The chapter discussed the development of a data dictionary that can be used in a distributed data-processing environment. A considerable amount of information was included on the operational aspects of DDP.

The intent of the chapter was to introduce the readers to an environment that has great potential for use because of the increasing reliability of data communications and security controls.

With the help of the fundamental information on DDP's and data dictionaries in this chapter, the reader can either develop a dictionary or select one using criteria developed from reading this chapter.

6

Data Dictionaries in Office Automation Environments

Introduction

The *electronic office* concept is not well defined, but the term generally refers to the use of electronic equipment to store, present, and communicate information rather than being limited to the use of paper media as our present office technology now requires. Although the electronic office may use paper as an adjunct or to interface with office personnel without electronic support, the paper technology plays a supporting role rather than a primary one.

Other terms have been used to refer to the concept of electronic office. These terms include "automated office," "peopleless office," and "office of the future."

An *electronic office* may be defined as one in which information, including text, data, and graphics, is kept in digital form in a computer. The electronic office has some or all of the following facilities:

- Word processing
- Text processing
- Electronic mail
- Intelligent copiers
- Teleconferencing
- Online storage, retrieval, and filing

An increasing number of organizations are merging electronic office workstations with their overall data-processing systems. It has been suggested that to obtain the full benefits, automated office technology must be integrated into the overall organization's information system. As concrete evidence of this, the devices used for electronic office workstations are becoming indistinguishable from computer terminals.

A wide range of functions exist in electronic office workstations. Functions range from data entry to global editing with data received from the computer system.

A workstation interrelates the use of dictation equipment, text-editing displays, printers, and communications equipment. Information is stored in a variety of media including tape cassettes, floppy disks, and cartridge disks. Output media include magnetic media, printers, phototypesetting equipment, and communications. Functions performed include word processing and text editing for document generation; communications and interchange of files, reports, and documents; and data entry for data processing.

Data-processing and text- or word-processing technologies are converging rapidly and should be viewed as two pieces of the same integrated picture. The convergence of the two technologies is spurred by sharp decreases in hardware costs and improvements in communications and functions. The forcing function behind the merger of the two disciplines is the goal of creating a cohesive organization and a wide information-handling system. In the final analysis, much of the near-term motivation is to reduce cost through more efficient and effective use of the organization.

6.1 Technology Used in Electronic Office Workstations

The technology now used in the electronic office workstation includes:

- *Word processors.*   Keyboards and CRT's or printers which generate and edit documents electronically from storage
- *Intelligent copiers.*   Laser printers which accept binary coded information and produce alphanumeric and graphic images on paper
- *Facsimile.*   Devices which scan documents, transmit the information over a communications system, and reproduce the documents at the receiving end
- *Electronic mail.*   Systems which accept messages, usually from a terminal and addressed to one or more individuals, and transmit the messages electronically to those individuals, usually at other terminals
- *Home terminals.*   Computer terminals used in the home

- *Photocomposition.*   Typesetting systems used to generate plates for printing

- *Computer output microfilm.*   Devices which generate alphanumeric and graphic images on microfilm based on output from computers

6.2   Improvements in Office Personnel Support

A workstation consisting of the elements listed in section 6.1 can greatly improve the productivity of support personnel, for example in document preparation and dissemination. In particular, the following steps are made more efficient:

- *Document generation.*   Local storage provides for recall of information, and the CRT allows for easy editing and correcting.

- *Mailing.*   Conventional mailing is replaced by a system in which text or image information is sent over a digital communication system to an "electronic mailbox" for each addressee. This is much cheaper and eliminates the current delay of several days in mailing systems. It enables a principal to receive mail and send messages anywhere in the world that a telephone and "mailbox" are available.

- *Filing.*   Documents can be filed under several identifiers (date, topic, customer) and then accessed by conventional data-retrieval techniques, thus eliminating the time, expense, and bulk of conventional storage cabinets.

- *Forms.*   Rather than being preprinted, forms are held in digital form in mass storage and are called up on the CRT screen as required. The blanks also can be filled in right on the screen.

6.3   Network Architecture for Office Automation

With the advent of office systems, the need for cross-vendor standardization in protocols for computer networks has become apparent.

A network architecture must therefore define the access paths, procedures, and rules which enable devices and people not only to be connected to each other but to actually communicate. The distinction between the phrases "to be connected" and "to communicate" is important. Two workstations connected to one another are of little value to their users if all they can do is exchange a meaningless stream of bits.

To attempt to address this problem in the industry, various standards organizations are working to adopt standard protocols. The next few sections describe two of these protocols.

6.4 The Open Systems Interconnection Model

Probably the most important effort, from the standpoint of strategic planning for office systems in user organizations is the International Standards Organization (ISO) Reference Model for Open Systems Interconnection (OSI). The 7-layer model specifies an architecture for open systems interconnection. The ISO and other standards organizations are continuing to work to define these protocols. Because the ISO's model is a reference point for much of the other standardization work under way, understanding it is important.

The term "open systems" refers to the ability of heterogeneous vendors' equipment to communicate through a network. The OSI model consists of 7 layers that divide the communications process into acts of related services. Each layer is based on lower layers and provides services for higher layers in the model.

The model helps to clarify and explain the various networks and standards which exist. For example, the lower layers of the OSI model are the same as the X.25 standard which is agreed upon widely. As a result, protocols at these levels are defined and effectively adopted. However, protocols at the higher levels are more complex.

Another example is IBM's SNA network which has protocols corresponding to roughly the fifth layer of the OSI model.

The OSI model can provide a basis for developing an overall network strategy. It provides a model to understand the current networks.

6.5 Local Area Networks

There have been many traditional "local" networks in offices. Computer networks have enabled various terminals, printers, and other peripherals to be connected with a central computer. A second type of local network has been the office telephone network, in which telephones are all attached to a private branch exchange (PBX).

With the motion toward desktop computing, we have seen the rise of a new generation of networks called "local area networks" (LAN's).

6.6 The Private Branch Exchange

The first phase of PBX's saw vendors providing the capability to switch data as well as voice using a digital PBX. Used in this limited fashion, the PBX can provide a natural, low-risk bridge to networking. If data and voice are multiplexed together on twisted-pair wire, the bandwidth is relatively low but adequate for most workstation requirements.

There are a number of problems with this approach. The additional load may overburden existing telephone circuits on which capacity may already be a problem. The network is vulnerable to catastrophic failure because of total reliance on the PBX. Then too, computer-to-computer communications, graphics transfer, and video cannot be handled using this approach because of the low bandwidth of twisted-pair wire.

The second phase of PBX approaches to local area networks was announced by many leading vendors in 1983. In this development, the PBX star is integrated with other network types or different topologies, transmission media, and access methods.

In this phase, the PBX is central to the LAN. A number of facilities can be attached to this PBX, including:

- *Telephones containing an add-on data module (ADM).* A computer terminal or intelligent workstation can be connected to the PBX through this ADM.

- *Microcomputers with attached peripherals.*

- *Computer terminals with limited local intelligence.*

- *Display telephones.* Two telephone lines (one for voice and one for data) go to the switch.

- *Coaxial cable LAN's.* Consisting of a baseband bus attached through a transceiver to the PBX. Various devices hand off the network, including communications processors which can provide access to other facilities, such as the company mainframe.

6.7 Functional Areas in Office Automation

This section describes functional areas in the automated office that can be readily adapted to data dictionary usage. These areas include:

- Storage and retrieval
- Message transmittal
- Document transmittal
- Document routing
- Distribution
- Tracking
- Scheduling
- Analysis
- Data entry
- Protection

- File maintenance
- Search

6.8   The Data Dictionary's Role in Storage and Retrieval

The data dictionary can be used to store definitions of storage data and the authorization required to retrieve that data.

In the areas of message and document transmittal as well as distribution of reports, the data dictionary can be used as a repository of text information to effect the transmittal. The dictionary formats can be altered to accommodate metadata about documents for transmittal.

The dictionary described in Chapter 3 can be readily adapted for use in the office automation environment. At present there are no manufacturer's data dictionaries which serve the office automation environment.

Security and Integrity of Data Dictionaries

Introduction

This chapter considers the security, privacy, and integrity of data dictionaries. The topic will be approached in two ways:

- The security of the data dictionary as an object exposed to a threat
- The security that the data dictionary can provide to objects, defined as entries

7.1 Definitions of Security, Privacy, and Integrity

Data security is defined as the procedural and technical measures required to:

- Prevent any deliberate denial of service
- Prevent unauthorized access, modification, use, and dissemination of data stored or processed in a computer system
- Protect the system in its entirety from physical harm

The access-control requirements are particularly important in time-shared and multiprogrammed systems in which multiple users must be prevented from interfering with each other and from gaining unauthorized access to each other's data or programs.

Computer privacy concerns the moral and legal requirements to protect data from unauthorized access and dissemination. Therefore the issues involved in computer privacy are political decisions regarding who may have access to what and who may disseminate what. On the other hand, the issues involved in *computer security* are procedures and safeguards for enforcing the privacy decisions.

Privacy issues affect all aspects of computer security because of legislative measures enacted. With due consideration of its social implications, legislation for computer privacy determines the type of information collected and by whom, the type of access and dissemination, the subject's rights, the penalties, and the licensing matter.

Integrity is a measure of the quality and reliability of the data on which computer-based information systems depend. Many computerized databases in use today suffer from high error rates in the data they receive, and consequently are riddled with bad and incorrect data. This situation can render even the most efficient and sophisticated system useless.

Privacy of personal information on individuals maintained in computerized record-keeping systems is an issue that concerns the computer community. It addresses the individual's rights regarding the collection and storage of information about their persons and activities, as well as the processing, dissemination, storage, and use of this information in making decisions about the individuals involved.

In 1973 the U.S. Department of Health, Education, and Welfare proposed several actions that should be taken to help protect individual privacy. This report proposed the following fundamental principles of fair information practice to guide the development of regulations and laws concerning privacy.

1. The existence of record-keeping systems that include personal data cannot be kept secret.

2. Individuals must have a way to find out what personal information about themselves is in a record and how it is used.

3. Individuals must have a way to prevent personal information obtained for one purpose from being used or made available for other purposes without their consent.

4. Individuals must have a way to correct or amend any records of identifiable information about themselves.

5. Any organization creating, maintaining, using, or disseminating records of identifiable personal data must assume the reliability of the data for its intended use and must take reasonable precautions to prevent misuse of the data.

Guidelines and procedures may be established for accountability, levels of control, types of control, rules, and checklists. Preventive measures and recovery from internal threats and external intrusions also form part of data security. For threats and intrusions, the causes, effects, and means must be studied. More difficult aspects of research on data security include risk analysis, threat analysis, assessment, and insurance. By knowing the risks involved, data security may be expressed in terms of quantitative indicators, cost factors, and options.

7.2 Conducting a Threat Analysis

A *threat* is defined as that which has the potential to menace, abuse, or harm. A threat can either modify or destroy the functional purpose of an object, and hence is a source of potential danger. In the context of our discussion of threat analysis and data security, the term "threat" will be used to mean the danger to which data is exposed.

Threat analysis is defined as the methodology employed to assess the level of the system's security and the protection mechanisms in place to counter the threats. Threat analysis is also useful in designing cost-effective security systems. A good threat analysis is an important element in the review of security needs. Together with an analysis of vulnerability, it provides the basic data needed to assess the risks. Even if threats are not expressed in probabilistic terms, their existence should be recognized and priority ratings should be assigned.

The threats considered in this chapter are limited to those faced by the data. We will not consider those threats to physical security which usually are countered by the installation of physical preventive measures. In this category of threats are fire hazards, illegal entry into a specific computer installation, and hardware failure.

The methodology most frequently used and employed in studies which produced most of the data for this chapter is the checklist method. This approach consists essentially of asking a series of questions to determine what protection measures are in place to counter threats against specific objects. In using this methodology, considerable attention should be devoted to planning the questionnaire and the follow-up interviews with respondents. The researcher should set specific objectives and clearly measurable goals for each associated task. The scheduling and coordinating of interviews with the various respondents should be planned carefully.

7.3 Examples of Survey Questions

The objects selected for the study may include the data dictionary, program libraries, source and object modules for languages such as Cobol and Fortran, and data files.

The questions asked in the survey will seek to determine what protection exists to counter the following categories of threats:

- Unauthorized access to libraries
- Unauthorized manipulation of library members
- Authorized users browsing the library without approval
- Unauthorized use of utilities
- Destruction of the storage medium
- Unauthorized distribution or exposure of reports or outputs
- Unauthorized copying or altering of libraries
- Illegal deletion of stored data
- Passing of sensitive data by authorized users to unauthorized users
- Unauthorized access to residues
- Unauthorized use of terminal to access data
- Collusion of employees
- Denial of access to system resources

7.4   Protection Mechanisms

Protection mechanisms are defined as the techniques used to safeguard an object against a particular threat. The mechanisms discussed here include

- Access management
- Privacy transformations
- Cryptographic controls
- Security kernels
- Access matrix
- Data dictionary

7.5   Access Management

These techniques are aimed at preventing unauthorized users from obtaining services from the system or gaining access to its files. The procedures involved are authorization, identification, and authentication. Authorization is given for certain users to enter the database and request certain types of information. Users attempting to enter the system must first identify themselves and their locations, and then authenticate the identification.

7.6   Privacy Transformations

Privacy transformations are techniques for concealing information by coding the data in user-processor communications or in files. Privacy transformations consist of sets of logical operations on the individual characters of the data. Privacy transformations break down into two general types—irreversible and reversible.

Irreversible privacy transformations include aggregation and random modification. In this case valid statistics can be obtained from such data, but individual values cannot be obtained.

Reversible privacy transformations are as follows:

- *Coding.*   Replacement of a group of words in one language by a word in another language.

- *Compression.*   Removal of redundancies and blanks from transmittal data.

- *Substitution.*   Replacement of letters in one or more items.

- *Transposition.*   Distortion of the sequence of letters in the ciphered text; all letters in the original text are retained in this technique.

- *Composite transformation.*   Combinations of the above methods.

7.7   Cryptographic Controls

Cryptographic transformations were recognized long ago as an effective protection mechanism in communication systems. In the past they were used mainly to protect information transferred through communication lines.

There is still much debate about the cost-benefit ratio of encrypting large databases. My experience with encryption indicates that the cost of producing clear text from large encrypted databases is prohibitive.

7.8   Security Kernels

Security kernels, as the name suggests, are extra layers of protection surrounding the operating system. The kernels are usually software programs which are used to test for authenticity and to either authorize or deny all user requests to the operating system.

A request to the operating system to execute a task or retrieve data from the database is routed to the security kernel, where the request is examined to determine if the user is authorized to access the requested data. If all checks are passed, the request is transmitted to the operating system, which then executes the request.

7.9   Access Matrix

The *access matrix* is an internal protection mechanism built into the operating system. It is essentially a set of tables that indicate who has access to what data. The access matrix consists of the following components:

- Objects that are to be protected
- Subjects seeking access to those objects
- Different protection levels for each object
- Rules that determine how the subjects access each object
- A monitor that mediates all access of a subject to an object
- Directories containing information about objects and subjects

The interaction between the subjects and objects can be represented by an access-control matrix (see Figure 7.1). The protectable objects are the row components of the matrix. The subjects seeking access to the objects are the column components of the matrix. Each entry in the access matrix determines the access rights of the subject to the object and is defined as the access attribute in the model. The access matrix model is dynamic enough to include any class of objects or subjects

	Employee Name	Employee Address	Employee Phone No.	Employee S.I.N.	Employee Education	Employee Salary	Employee Medical	Employee Position
Personnel	11	11	11	11	11	11	11	11
Accounting	01	01	01	01	00	00	00	01
Marketing	00	00	00	00	00	00	00	00
Purchasing	00	00	00	00	00	00	00	00
DBA	11	11	11	11	11	11	11	11
Operations	10	10	10	10	10	10	10	10
Programmer	11	11	11	11	11	11	11	11
Clerical	01	01	01	00	00	00	00	00

Legend
01– Read
11– Read and write
00– No access
10– Write only

Figure 7.1   Typical access matrix

within the data-processing environment. Each object is placed in a class determined by its level of protection.

In Figure 7.1 the 11 in the first row and first column indicates that personnel can read and write the employee name in the database. The 00 in row 3 and column 2 indicates that marketing has no access right to the employee address. If marketing tried to gain access, the operating system should deny access, on the basis of a warning from the access matrix.

7.10 Protecting the Data Dictionary

The protection mechanisms described in this chapter can be used to protect the data dictionary from illegal entry and from changes in existing material.

In today's environment, passwords alone are not effective tools for protecting the data dictionary. Many installations are using authorization tables as protection mechanisms, and several others are considering encryption.

7.11 The Data Dictionary as a Protection Mechanism

The data dictionary can be used in the database environment to protect the organization's data. Entries in the dictionary can be used to indicate who has access rights to what data and who can update or alter that data. It can also be used to indicate who has responsibility for creating and changing definitions. The dictionary described in Chapter 3 has entries which can be used as protection mechanisms.

8

Database Design Using the Data Dictionary

Introduction

This chapter presents an overview of database design and the role the data dictionary can play in the development of systems using design methodologies.

Database design is the process of arranging the data fields needed by one or more applications into an organized structure. That structure must foster the required relationships among the fields while conforming to the physical constraints of the particular DBMS in use. The two parts of the process are, first, logical database design and, second, physical database design.

Logical database design is an implementation-independent exercise that is performed on the fields and relationships needed for one or more applications. Physical database design is an implementation-dependent exercise that takes the results of logical database design and further refines them according to the characteristics of the particular database management system in use.

Careful database design is essential for a variety of reasons including data redundancy, application performance, data independence, data security, and ease of programming. All are important factors in the data-processing environment, and all can be affected adversely by a poor database design.

8.1 Review of Existing Methodologies

This section presents two of the most common database design methodologies. The first methodology, data normalization and data structuring, is representative of a class of methods that take as input a list of fields and the associations among those fields.

The second method, the entity-relationship method, is representative of the class of methods that take entities and relationships as input.

Database design using the entity-relationship model lists the entity types involved and the relationships among them. The philosophy of assuming that the designer knows what the entity types are at the outset is significantly different from the philsosophy behind the normalization-based approach.

The approach uses entity-relationship diagrams as illustrated in Figure 8.1. The rectangular boxes represent entity types, the diamond-shaped box represents a relationship between entities, and the circular figures represent attributes.

A more detailed discussion of the method is given in the following sections.

8.2   Detailed Discussion of Database Design

The process of developing a database structure from user requirements is called "database design." Most practitioners agree that there are two separate phases to the database design process: (1) the design of a logical database structure that is processible by DBMS and describes the user's view of data, and (2) the selection of a physical structure such as the indexed sequential or direct-access method of the intended DBMS. Other than the logical physical delineation, the overall structure of the design is not well defined.

Four basic components that are necessary to achieve a database design methodology are:

- A structured design process that consists of a series of steps in which one alternative among many is chosen

- Design techniques to perform the enumeration required, as stated previously, and evaluation criteria to select an alternative at each step

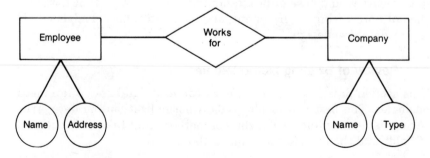

Figure 8.1 The entity-relationship diagram

- Information requirements for input to the design process as a whole and to each step of the design process.

- A descriptive mechanism to represent the information input and the results of each design step

Current database design technology shows many residual effects of its outgrowth from single-record file design methods. File design is primarily application-program-dependent since the data has been defined and structured in terms of individual applications that use them. The advent of DBMS revised the emphasis on data and program design approaches. The concept of the integrated database spanning multiple users was a direct result of the complex data-structuring capabilities that the DBMS afforded. Data can now be viewed as a corporate resource instead of as an adjunct to a program, and consequently should have an integrated-requirements orientation instead of a single-program orientation.

Achieving a design that results in an acceptable level of database performance for all has become a complex task. The database designer must be ever conscious of the cost-performance trade-offs associated with multiple users of a single integrated database. Potential savings of storage and expanded applicability of databases into corporate decision making should be accompanied by a critical analysis of potential degradation of service to some users. Such degradation is to be avoided if possible. Acceptable performance for all users should be the goal.

Another aspect of database design is flexibility. Databases that are bound too tightly to current applications may have too limited a scope for many corporate enterprises. Rapidly changing requirements and new data elements may result in costly program maintenance, a proliferation of temporary files, and increasingly poor performance. A meaningful overall database design process should allow for both integration and flexibility.

8.3 Inputs to the Design Process

The major classes of inputs to and result from the database design process are

General information requirements

Processing requirements

DBMS specifications

Operating system and hardware configurations

Application-program specifications

The major classes of results are

Logical database structure (users' view)

Storage structure (physical design)

The general information requirements represent various users' descriptions of the organization for which data is to be collected, the objective of the database, and the user's views of which data should be collected and stored in the database. These requirements are process-independent because they are not tied to any specific database management system or application. Database design based on these requirements is considered advantageous for long-term databases that must be adaptable to changing processing requirements.

Processing requirements consist of three distinguishable components: (1) specific data required for each application, (2) data volume and expected growth, and (3) processing frequencies for the number of times each application must be run per unit time. Each of these components is very important to a particular stage or step of the database design process.

Performance measures and performance constraints are also imposed on the database design. Typical constraints include upper bounds on response times to queries, recovery times from system crashes, and specific data needed to support certain security or integrity requirements.

Specific performance measures used to evaluate the final structure might include update, storage, and reorganization costs in addition to response requirements.

The three major outputs of the database design process are the logical database structure, the physical storage structure, and specifications for application programs based on those database structures and processing requirements. As a whole, these results may be considered the specification for the final database implementation.

8.4   The Entity-Relationship Methodology

As more and more organizations implement systems employing database technology, the need arises for better methodologies to design these databases. The methodology described here provides a means of mapping the entity model produced from the data-analysis phase to the DBMS-supported structure.

The ER approach requires four steps to produce a structure that is acceptable by the particular DBMS. These steps—data analysis, producing and optimizing the entity model, logical schema development, and physical database design process—are discussed below.

8.5   The Data-Analysis Phase

A fundamental part of ER methodology is the data-analysis phase concerned with identifying the data resources of an organization. Although methodologies for data analysis have stemmed from the need for a new approach to system design in a database environment, experience has shown that the concept of data analysis has a wider applicability, whether or not database software is involved. The approach to data analysis, the scale involved, and the emphasis placed on the various tasks that must be done depend very much on the objectives of the project.

Researchers indicate that data analysis is used to

1. Determine the fundamental data resources of an organization.

2. Permit the design of flexible file structures capable of supporting a number of related applications.

3. Aid application development or conversion by providing a fundamental understanding of the data involved.

4. Form a basis for data control, security, and auditing of the resulting applications and systems.

5. Organize all relevant facts concerning the organization's data.

6. Aid the unification of an organization by indicating the commonality between its departments and data requirements.

7. Provide a basis for evaluating the structuring capability of competing DBMS's.

8. Identify the entities that are relevant to solve the existing data-processing problem.

9. Determine the relationships among these entities.

10. Establish data and process definitions in a data dictionary.

11. Produce the entity model.

The primary interest in data analysis is providing a sound basis for database design. Data analysis provides a disciplined approach to cataloging the existing data in terms of the entities and relationships it represents. Without such an understanding of that part of the organization being analyzed, it is difficult to establish whether and where a database could be installed efficiently. Data analysis provides a very effective means of communicating with non-data-processing users, as it deals only with things that the users are familiar with and not with objects such as files and records.

The data analysis sometimes is referred to as "requirements formulation and analysis," which involves the establishment of organization objectives, derivation of specific database requirements from these objectives or directly from management personnel, and documentation of these requirements in a form that is agreeable to management and database designers.

8.6   Conducting the Data-Analysis Phase

Data analysis is best conducted by a team of individuals drawn from the user community, the systems-development department, data administration, and the corporate standards department.

The data-analysis team may be involved in the project-requirements analysis phase if that phase is limited to personal interviews with various levels of managers and key employees involved in the processing of goods, services, and data in the organization. The result of such interviews should be flow diagrams of the processes (e.g., illustrations of steps required to process an invoice and where in the organization these steps are taken) with which each employee is involved, an identification of the data elements associated with each process, interfaces between processes, and a verification that both interviewer and employee agree on the flow-model semantics. Specific objectives and database requirements should be obtained at the highest possible level in the organization.

First the data-analysis team identifies the entities that are needed to solve the problems defined by the users. During the initial stages of data analysis, not all the attributes of each entity may be known. However, as each attribute is determined, the team should document the attribute's definition and role in an appropriate data dictionary.

8.7   The Entity Model

During the data-analysis phase, the major entities and their relationships are determined. These entities and their relationships are represented by models called "entity models." The model is a diagrammatical representation of the relationship between the entity classes. The representation allows us to include only those entities that are required to solve the particular data-processing problem. The entity model is essentially a real-world view of the organizational data in terms of entities, attributes, and relationships.

During the entity-modeling phase, the most significant entity classes and relationships are defined. But inevitably a model will be revised, modified, or extended as a result of new knowledge about the entities being discovered. The model is used by the analysis team to

1. Reduce redundancy in the relationships.

2. Determine which entities are significant to the model and to the user's requirements.

3. Resolve nonbinary relationships between entities. Figure 8.2 illustrates an entity model.

8.8   Role of the Data Dictionary in Data Analysis

The data dictionary's role in database design first appears in the data-analysis phase of the design. During this phase all the entities and their attributes that are identified are documented in the data dictionary.

The data dictionary described in previous chapters of this text can be used to document these entities and their attributes. The attribute and entity class definitions can be used in this case.

8.9   Role of the Data Dictionary in Entity Modeling

The data dictionary can be used as a tool to document all the details of the entity model. The entity model is primarily a diagrammatic representation of the entities and their relationships. The entity class and logical schema definitions of the data dictionary described in this book can be used to document the entity model.

8.10   Logical Schema Design

The *logical schema* may be defined as the mapping of the entity model into the constructs provided by the DBMS—for example, the mapping of the entity model into an IMS construct. In general the logical schema indicates how the model will be stored and accessed. In the design of the logical schema, some restructuring of the model and changes to conform to the DBMS may be necessary.

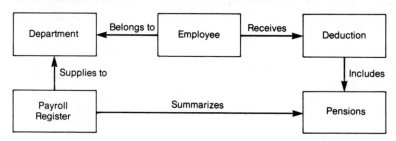

Figure 8.2   Entity model for paycheck processing

The logical schema definition of the data dictionary described in this book can be used to document the logical schema phase of database design.

8.11 Role of the Data Dictionary in Physical Design

The details of physical design depend very much on the characteristics of the DBMS chosen for the database design.

In an IMS environment, the physical design includes the following selections:

- Physical databases and types of logical relationships, whether unidirectionally or bidirectionally physically paired
- Access methods, whether HISAM, HIDAM, or HDAM
- Segments and hierarchical structures and data representation, including type and size
- Secondary indices
- Types of pointers in relationship

The logical group and IMS database definitions of the data dictionary described in the book can be used to document the results of physical database design.

In addition, volume and usage statistics necessary for the ordering of database segments and for determination of storage estimates can be documented in the data dictionary.

8.12 The Data Dictionary as a Directory

The data dictionary can be used as a directory to point to the physical location of the stored data in the database.

For example, the "external parameters" entry of the data dictionary described in this book can be used as a directory to point to the stored IMS data.

9

Developing
Data Dictionary
Standards

Introduction

The *data dictionary* is often defined as data about data. It contains names, descriptions, edit specifications, access rules, and other information on usage for each data element. The data dictionary may contain conventions for data naming and for standards and procedures regarding the content of the database.

The data dictionary can be used in an active mode to cluster attributes into entity classes, entity classes into an entity model, and the entity model into logical schemas, from which the physical databases are built. The data dictionary can be used as a documentation tool to check the accuracy of existing documentation. As a powerful tool used by internal auditors, it can audit and monitor application systems, access to stored data, and access violations. The data dictionary can also interface actively with the organization's computer operating system to deny access to unauthorized users.

In a passive mode the data dictionary can be used to identify and notify affected users of changes in existing data definitions. In an active mode it can determine and control users and use of shared data. The data dictionary can be used to facilitate data integration and reduce redundancy in data storage. It can interface with the operating system to produce access statistics that will enable the physical database designers to tune and reorganize the database.

9.1 Categories of Data Dictionary Standards

There are two types of data-related standards for data dictionaries: data definition standards and data format conformance.

"Data definition" refers to a standard way of describing data. One example is the naming of the data. The naming standard may be in the form of rigid rules or established conventions for assigning names to data entities. All user areas within the enterprise will know that, for instance, the data element "customer name"—used in files, programs, and reports—means the same throughout the enterprise.

"Data format conformance" is content-related. It means that a data element, in addition to having the same name throughout the enterprise, also must conform to a common set of format rules for the data element, to retain the same meaning. Moreover, these rules must be accepted throughout the enterprise. For example, all data elements involving "date" should have the same format throughout the enterprise—and only that format should be assigned. Similarly, if codes are to be used throughout the enterprise, these must be uniform. If an acceptable code for a state is a 2-letter code, that must be the universally accepted code in the enterprise, and no other code, whether 2-, 3-, or 4-letter, should be used.

9.2 Standard Formats for Data Dictionary Entries

Standards are required for the format and content used in defining and describing meta-entities of the data dictionary. This means setting standards for the type of information that must be collected for each entry type and, most important, for the conventions that must be observed in defining these attributes. In effect, this amounts to defining a set of standards for methods of preparing attribute, entity, and relationship descriptions.

There are a number of general guidelines for establishing a standard. Several standard entries were described in previous chapters of this book. A typical standard entry for a data element is given in Figure 9.1. A data element may be described in terms of the attributes in this figure.

9.3 Standards for Programs Interfacing with a Data Dictionary

Data dictionary standards for programming interface basically fall into the area of the structure of the "call" statement from the programming language to the dictionary package.

Other standards in this area will indicate how high-level languages will use the data dictionary to build file structures and record layouts. They will also indicate how these languages will access the dictionary itself.

Data Element	Definition
Identification number	A 7–character unique identifier beginning with ELXXXXX.
Designator	A short name composed of the keywords of the DESCRIPTION.
Programming name	An abbreviated form of the DESIGNATOR using only approved abbreviations. Example: LEGL–CUST–NAME.
Description	A narrative explanation of the data element; the first sentence must identify the real–world entity being described. The second sentence may expand on usage characteristics. Example: The name of a customer, which is the legal name. It may not be the commonly used name. It is usually derived from legal papers.

Figure 9.1   Sample standard for data element description

9.4   Security Standards

Standards for access rules and controls will indicate who can access the dictionary, how the dictionary contents will be accessed, and whether the contents will be accessed in their original form or as copies.

Standards in the area of security will cover the use of the data dictionary as a protection mechanism and the entries that must be made in the data dictionary to achieve those standards.

10

Performance Indicators of Data Dictionaries

Introduction

The performance of a data dictionary can be measured in a number of ways, including:

Types of reports produced

Ability to produce ad hoc reports

Ease of entering and retrieving data

Ability to check the accuracy, consistency, and completeness of entries

Ability to associate attributes with entities and entities with logical schemas

Interaction of processes and data elements

The next several sections will describe how performance can be measured in each of the above areas.

10.1 Types of Reports Produced

Users of data dictionaries can measure the performance of the data dictionary by the types of reports generated by the dictionary. The dictionary must produce reports beyond the standard glossaries and definitions that are produced by most standard dictionaries.

Reports which allow the user to relate entities and data elements, the percentage of elements with definitions, and reports that give volume and other user statistics are recommended for all data dictionaries.

10.2   Ability to Produce Ad Hoc Reports

The data dictionary must be able to produce ad hoc reports from queries. These reports should include reports of attribute values for user-specified names, privacy and security level of dictionary entries, frequency of use and execution of certain definitions, and the control requirements of attributes and entities.

10.3   Ease of Entering and Retrieving Data

The data dictionary will be judged by the ease with which users can enter and retrieve data. If users can enter data using a user-friendly teleprocessing monitor, e.g., TSO, and can retrive data in a similar manner, then the use of that dictionary will certainly increase. For example, a single command should produce results.

10.4   Ability to Check Accuracy of Contents

A user should be able to check the accuracy, consistency, and completeness of data dictionary entries. In the area of consistency, names and labels should be consistent with those used outside the data dictionary environment. Definitions should be complete and accurate.

10.5   Ability to Associate Attributes with Entities

The data dictionary user should be able to associate attributes with their relevant entities in both a forward and a backward direction. That is, the dictionary should, if given an entity, list all the related attributes of that entity and should, if given an attribute, list the entity and all other related attributes.

10.6   Interaction of Processes and Data Elements

The dictionary should be in a position to provide a matrix of processes and the attributes that are referenced by them. It should also indicate what attributes are never referenced by processes.

10.7   Data Dictionary Summary Reports

The summary reports should provide status on the information and entries in the data dictionary. For example, the user should be able to get a count of each entry along with a number and percentage of each entry having

Entry	Count	Number with DESC	Percent with DESC	Number with Synonyms	Percent with Synonyms
Undefined	1	0		0	
Attribute	12	0		0	
Entire	50	45	90	30	60
Group	100	90	90	80	80
Logical schema	80	40	50	20	25

Figure 10.1   Data dictionary summary reports

- Synonyms
- Descriptions

The summary reports are useful in determining whether any entries are classified as undefined. A sample of this performance indicator is shown in Figure 10.1.

Case Histories of Data Dictionary Usage

Introduction

The case histories outlined in this part are taken from actual companies' accounts of their use of data dictionaries. Every effort is made to protect the identity of those companies. The data presented here is unedited.

CASE HISTORY 1

The DB/DC Data Dictionary

A set of data bases that are used to store and access information about an installation's data processing resources.

The dictionary contains data *about* data.

Subject Categories

- IBM defined
  - Systems/subsystems
  - Jobs
  - Programs/modules
  - Data bases
  - PSBs/PCBs
  - Segments/records
  - Data elements
- Installation defined
  - Business function
  - Logical transactions
  - Data classes
  - Physical transactions
  - Reports
  - OS files
  - Reusable packets

Information on Subjects

- Name
  - Unique/meaningful

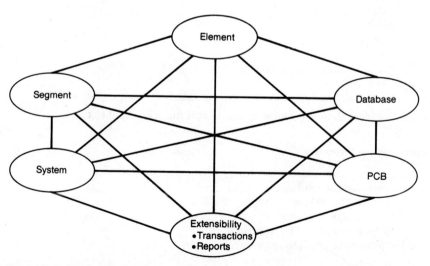

Figure 11.1 Dictionary databases

- Primary/alias
- 1 to 31 positions/language (BAL/Cobol/PL/I)
- Attributes
  - Depends on category
  - Language of program
  - Length of a data element
- Description
  - Descriptive name (user name) on line one
  - Any descriptive matter starting on line three
  - 999 lines of 72 positions each
- User data
  - Provision for five separate types
  - Audit trail
  - Edit criteria
  - System identification
  - Reusable packet information
  - Application related information
- Relationships
  - To other entities
  - System to job
  - Job to program
- Relationship data
  - Information about the relationship between two entities
  - Indicative key (data element within segment)

Identification of Subjects (Dictionary Name)

- Components of name
  - Status code
    - Identifies status of entity
  - Subject category (code)
    - Identifies category
  - Name
    - Primary name on the dictionary
  - Occurrences
    - Distinguishes different physical attributes
- All the identifiers are required while working with a subject (Subject name)

Accessing the Dictionary

- Interactive on-line facility
  - Screens for each subject
  - Prompting for action
  - Screen to screen access
  - Available through TSO terminals
  - Used for entry/update/retrieval
- Batch forms
  - Card image

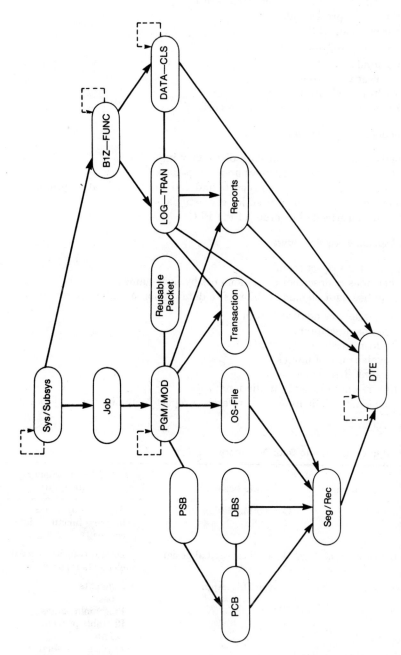

Figure 11.2 Data dictionary relationship diagram

135

- Identifying control info on each record
- Bulk data processing
- For entering only
- Available through TSO
- Commands
  - Interactive on-line
  - Within batch processing
  - Example: scan, change name, report

Procedure for Documentation

- Application group fills out data dictionary input forms
- Data dictionary group reviews and enters data
- Data dictionary group runs reports and delivers to application group
- Input forms may also be used for corrections
- Order of entities follow order of the PLC

Data Element Entry Procedure

- Application project team
  - Identifies & describes data elements by user name
  - Supplies data element I/P forms to data dictionary administration
- Data dictionary administration
  - Assigns descriptors
  - Performs redundancy analysis
  - Develops Cobol names
  - Assigns BAL name
  - Enters data elements in dictionary
  - Sends data element & cross reference report to application project team

Entry of Information into Data Dictionary

Project life cycle	Data base design	Data dictionary documentation
Feasibility	Conceptual design	System/subsystems business functions data classes
Functional analysis	Detailed conceptual design	Logical transactions data elements reports
System design	Logical DB design	Segments Jobs Program/modules Reusable packets OS files Physical transactions
Implementation	Physical DB design	Data bases PSB's/PCB's

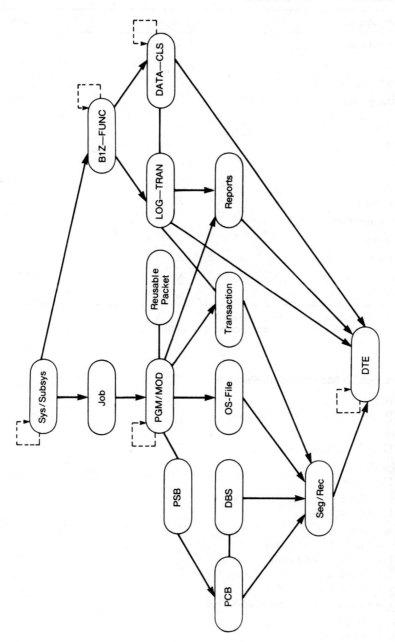

Figure 11.3 Data dictionary relationship diagram

137

Responsibilities for Subject Categories

Subject categories	Appl. proj. team	DBA
System/subsystem	X	—
Job	X	—
Program/module	X	—
Reusable packet	X	X
Data base	—	X
PSB/PCB	—	X
Segment	—	X
Record	X	—
Data element	X(P)	X(S)
Business function	X	—
Transaction	X	—
Data class	X	—
Report	X	—
OS file	X	—

P = Primary responsibility for definition
S = Secondary responsibility—provides required assistance

Information on Subjects—Data Elements

- Names
  - Primary and at least one alias
- Attributes
  - Length/picture/usage
- Description
  - User name
  - Descriptor
  - Free form text
- User data
  - User data 1—audit trail
  - User data 2—edit criteria
  - User data 3—system acronym
  - User data 4—unused
  - User data 5—application specified
- Relationships
- Relationship data

WDA Class Words

Word	Symbol	Definition
Address	A	Mailing address
Amount	$	Dollars and cents
Code	C	Concise way of expressing multiple choice
Count (quantity)	Q	Quantity of anything except money
Date	D	Calendar date
Flag	F	On/off, yes/no indicator
Group	G	Group element
Key	K	Data processing key
Name	N	Data which identified specific entities
Number	#	Alpha-numeric data which identifies the specific entities
Percent	%	Ratio between data expressed as a percentage
Time	T	Time of day—also duration
Text (words)	W	Free-form text

"OF" Language

¢ Of
* Which is/are
& And
' Or
/ By/within/per

WDAR003   DB/LC Data Dictionary Report

Wholesale Data Administration   Data Element Descriptor Redundancy Report

Duplicate	Status code	Element name	Descriptor
	L	CBL-CHRG-AMT	$ CBL-CHRG
	L	CDS-ACCT-CLRG-AMT	$ CDS-CLRG/ACCT
	L	CUST-CDS-TOT-CLRG-AMT	$ CDS-CLRG/CUST
	L	WDDA-ACCT-CDS-TOT-CLRG-AMT	$ CDS-CLRG/WDDA-ACCT
	A	ACCEPT-OUT-CHRG-AMT	$ CHGR*OUT
	L	CHK-DR-TOT	$ CHK-DR
	A	COMMIT-CHRG-AMT	$ CHRG COMMIT
	A	FRGN-CURNCY-COMMIT-CHRG-AMT	$ CHRG COMMIT*FRGN-CURNCY
	J	CHRG-OFF-AMT	$ CHRG-OFF
	J	CHRG-OFF-TOT	$ CHRG-OFF*TOT

```
******* L   CLSNG-AVAIL-CR-SUBTOT           $ CLSNG-AVAIL*CR
        L   CLSNG-AVAIL-CR-TOT              $ CLSNG-AVAIL*CR
******* L   CLSNG-AVAIL-DR-SUBTOT           $ CLSNG-AVAIL*DR
        L   CLSNG-AVAIL-DR-TOT              $ CLSNG-AVAIL*DR
******* L   CLSNG-AVAIL-SUBTOT              $ CLSNG-BAL*AVAIL
        L   CLSNG-AVAIL-TOT                 $ CLSNG-BAL*AVAIL
        L   1-DAY-FLT-CR-SUBTOT             $ CLSNG-BAL*CR*1-DAY-FLT
        L   2-OR-MOR-DAY-FLT-CR-SUBTOT      $ CLSNG-BAL*CR*2-OR-MOR-DAY-FLT
        L   1-DAY-FLT-DR-SUBTOT             $ CLSNG-BAL*DR*1-DAY-FLT
        L   2-OR-MOR-DAY-FLT-DR-SUBTOT      $ CLSNG-BAL*DR*2-OR-MOR-DAY-FLT
******* L   1-DAY-FLT-SUBTOT                $ CLSNG-BAL*1-DAY-FLT
        L   1-DAY-FLT-TOT                   $ CLSNG-BAL*1-DAY-FLT
        L   2-OR-MOR-DAY-FLT-SUBTOT         $ CLSNG-BAL*2-OR-MOR-DAY-FLT
******* L   1-DAY-FLT-DR-SUBTOT             $ CLSNG-BAL*DR*1-DAY-FLT
        L   2-OR-MOR-DAY-FLT-TOT            $ CLSNG-BAL*2-OR-MOR-DAY-FLT
        L   CLSNG-CR-BK-SUBTOT              $ CLSNG-BK*CR
```

Keyword Glossary

Keyword	Abbreviation	System ID	Description
TRANSMISSION	TRNMSN		
TRUST	TRUST		A fiduciary or agent function.
TYPE	TYPE		Kind, class, etc.
UNALLOCATED	UNALLO		Undetermined availability
UNDER	UNDER		
UNEARNED	UNEARNED		Describes fees collected at loan inception
UNIDENTIFIED	UNID		Describes funds of unknown availability and float.
UNIFORM CUSTOMS CODE	UCC		
UNIT	UNIT		
UNITED STATES GOVERNMENT	USG		The United States of America and territories.
UNITED STATES OF AMERICA	US		
UPDATE	UPD		To add to, change, or delete data
USER	USR		
USURY	USRY		Used in the context of "usury rate" to indicate the maximum interest rate allowed by law.
VALUE	VAL		Monetary worth—as in face value. Describes dollar value of collateral.
VERBAL	VBL		
VERSION	VERS		Used to describe (usually) successive variations or updates.
VIEW	VIEW		
VOSTRO	VOSTRO		Used by a depository bank to describe an account maintained with it by a bank in a foreign country. An account a foreign bank has with MHT.
VOYAGE	VOY		
WDDA	WDDA		Wholesale demand deposit accounting system

Data Dictionary
Reports References Guide

Reports

- Data element
  - For a status code
  - For a system
- Cross reference
  - For a system
  - By Cobol name or user name
- Data base/segment/field
- Assembler/Cobol/user name
  - For a data base
- System contents
  - System/subsystem/job/program
- System summary
  - System/program/DB/file/report/physical transaction
- Program relationship
  - Program/module/DB/file/reusable packet/physical transaction
- Business function
  - System/business function
- Business function/transaction summary
  - System/business function/logical transaction
- Automatically sent to data dictionary users
  - All other reports should be requested by submitting 'report request form'

Business Function/Transaction Report

System Name: (K, S, TEST–REPORTS–SYSTEM, 0)

```
SYS (K, S. TEST-REPORTS-SYSTEM, 0)
```
```
  BIZ_FUNC (K,,BUSINESS-FUNCTION-1,0)
```
   Business function 1 description lines

```
  BIZ_FUNC (K,,BUSINESS-FUNCTION-2,0)
```
   Business function 2 description lines

```
  BIZ_FUNC (K,,BUSINESS-FUNCTION-3,0)
```
   Business function 3 description lines
   This business function has no sub functions

```
  LOG_TRAN (K,,LOGICAL-TRANSACTION-8,0)
```
   Description lines for logical transaction 8
   A clear concise definition of the logical transaction

```
  BIZ_FUNC (K,,BUSINESS-FUNCTION-4,0)
```
   Business function 4 description lines
   This business function has no sub-functions

But it does have two logical transactions

LOG_TRAN (K,,Logical-TRANSACTION-9,0)
Description lines for logical transaction 9

LOG_TRAN (K,,LOGICAL-TRANSACTION-10,0)
Description lines for logical transaction 10

WDA0020A End of dictionary report

WDA DB/DC Data Dictionary Report

Worldwide Multibank
Description Cross Reference Report by Cobol Name

COBOL NAME: ACCT-BAL-CNTL-DATA
    USER NAME: Account control balance data overflow
    ASSEMBLER NAME: ACTBALCD
    DESCRIPTION: This is a group element which occurs
                  25 times

COBOL NAME: ACCT-BAL-CHTL-DATA-OVFL
    USER NAME: Account control balance data overflow
    ASSEMBLER NAME: ACTBALCO
    DESCRIPTION: This is a group element which occurs
                  45 times

COBOL NAME: ACCT-BAL-CNTL-SEG-KEY
    USER NAME: Account control segment key
    ASSEMBLER NAME: ACBLCNSK
    DESCRIPTION: The key of the account control of
                  balance segment. The key breakdown is
                  used by the special accounts. Other
                  accounts use COB date complement
                  only as a non-unique key. This is a
                  group element containing:
                    COB-DT-CMPL
                    CURNCY-CODE
                    ACCT-NUM-SUF

COBOL NAME: ACCT-BLK-EFF-DT
    USER NAME: Block effective date
    ASSEMBLER NAME: ACBLEFFD
    DESCRIPTION: This is the COB date on which a
                  viewing block becomes effective.

COBOL NAME: ACCT-BLK-EXPIR-DT
    USER NAME: Block expiration date

WDA DB/DC Data Dictionary Report

Worldwide Multibank
Description Cross Reference Report by User Name

Format.

USER NAME: ACCOUNT CONTROL REPORTING STATUS CODE
> COBOL NAME: ACCT—CNTL—STAT—CODE
> ASSEMBLER NAME: ACCNSTCD
> DESCRIPTION: This code indicates the reporting status
> of an account by close of business date.
> The code values are used to monitor
> reporting timeliness and completeness.

USER NAME: ACCOUNT CONTROL SEGMENT KEY
> COBOL NAME: ACCT—BAL—CNTL—SEG—KEY
> ASSEMBLER NAME: ACBLCNSK
> DESCRIPTION: The key of the account control of
> balance segment. The key breakdown is
> used by the special accounts. Other
> accounts use COB date complement
> only as a non-unique key. This is a
> group element containing:
> > COB—DT—CMPL
> > CURNCY—CODE
> > ACCT—NUM—SUF

USER NAME: ACCOUNT DATA BY SERVICE
> COBOL NAME: ACCT—SVC—DATA
> ASSEMBLER NAME: ACTSVCDA
> DESCRIPTION: This is a group element which occurs
> ten times. It contains:
> > HIST—DATA—DAY—CNT
> > CUST—ACCT—SVC—TYPE—CNT

USER NAME: ACCOUNT EFFECTIVE DATE
> COBOL NAME: ACCT—FRST—VIEW—DT
> ASSEMBLER NAME: ACFRSVWD
> DESCRIPTION: The first date on which an account will
> become available to customers.

DB/DC Data Dictionary Report

DICTIONARY DATA BASE: DTE

DATA ELEMENT: LC ACCT—BAL—CNTL—DATA 0
> SECONDARY NAME: LA ACTBALCD 0
> ATTRIBUTES LENGTH: 00020

Contains	STARTING POS	BITSTART USE	
LC BAL—TYPE—CODE O	00001	O	
LC BAL—CPIR—IND O	00005	O	
LC BAL—AMT O	00006	O	
LC BAL—LAST—UPD—DT—TIME O	00013	O	

Segment name	STARTING POS	BST LEVEL	
LA ACCCBALP O	00031	O	NOT USED
Occurs 25 times			IN DBD

DESCRIPTION:
001 Account control balance data
002 G*COB
003 This is a group element which occurs 25 times.

DTEUSER1: 995 06/29/81 M.IVANOVIC, Add

DTEUSER2:

DTEUSER3: 001 WMB Worldwide Multibank

DTEUSER4:

DTEUSER5:

End-of-Report

W. D. A. System Contents Report

SYSTEM REPORT FOR: (K,S,TST—SUBSYSTEM—2,0)

SYS (K,S,TST—SUBSYSTEM—2,0)
This is the second subsystem in TST-MAJOR-SYSTEM
It has a complex structure.

SYSTEM (K,S,TST—MAJOR—SYSTEM,0)
This is a sample system definition.
It is used to provide test data for WDA software development

JOB (K,J,JOB—21—0)
This is the first job in TST-SUBSYSTEM—2
It has two programs related to it.

JOB (K,J,JOB—22,0)
This is the second job in subsystem—2
It is a complex structure
It contains two programs.

PROGRAM (K,G,PGM—1,0)
This is the first PGM contained in JOB—22
PROGRAM (K,G,PGM—22—1,0)
This is the second program in JOB 22.

WDA0020A end of dictionary report on 10/16/81 at 17:25:30.

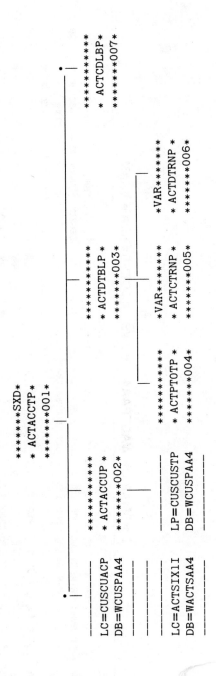

DMDMAP OF WACTPAA4   IMS/VS   ACCESS=HDAM VSAM

	LEVELS= 3	SEGMENTS= 7	DATA SET GROUPS= 1	
ID= 1 * WACTPA41	RANDOMIZING ROUTING=DFSHDC40	ROOT ANCHOR POINTS=	MAX RBN=	200 BYTES=
	PRIME DS LOG. RCD. LEN= 8185, BLOCKSIZE= 8192		SEGMENT LENGTH MAX= 830, MIN= 46	
	OSAM DS LOG. RCD. LEN= 8185, BLOCKSIZE= 8192		KEY LENGTH MAX= 19, MIN= 3	

```
                    C  P  P L L P P  L  L RULES PHYS.         SEG-NAME  D-B-NAME  FORM
                    R  FB P  T T P H C  C  C  C    N-SEQ         OR        OR      INSRT
SEG-NAME SC# LV PAR ..LEN..-FREQ-- TT P FB FB .F .L .F .L I D R  INSRT   FLD-NAME 1 LEN STRT PNTR RULES
                                                         P P V  LAST

ACTACCTP*  1  1  0   160 20000 X  X                    X  X  X  P P L LAST   SNDIXD                 FIX LEN
                                                                      *LC**  CUSCUACP WCUSPAA4 NONE LAST
                                                                      *LC**  ACTSIXII WACTSAA4 INDX LAST
                                                                      *FLD*  ACCTNUMB  12   1 CHARACTER
                                                                      *FLD*  WDDAACDT   6 102 CHARACTER
                                                                      *FLD*  DUPACTNM  12 132 CHARACTER
                                                                      *XFD*  SECSRFLD SECONDARY INDEXES FIELD

ACTACCUP*  2  2  1    32     0          X  X  X        P P L LAST   *LP**  CUSCUSTP WCUSPAA4 PHYS    FIX LEN
                                                                      *FLD*  CUSTRNUM   4   1 CHARACTER

ACTDTBLP*  3  2  1   176     0          XX                    LAST                                   FIX LEN
```

148

ACTPTOTP*	4	3	3	126	225	X
ACTCTRNP*	5	3	3	820	0	XX
ACTDTRNP*	6	3	3	820	0	XX
ACTCDLBP*	7	2	1	48	0	X

FLD	OPBBDTCM	6	1	CHARACTER
LAST				FIX LEN
FLD	PRODGCOD	3	1	CHARACTER
LAST				VAR LEN
FLD	TRNSEGKY	19	3	CHARACTER
FLD	TRNREFNM	12	10	CHARACTER
FLD	SSABBRNM	2	20	CHARACTER
FLD	REVSFLAG	1	22	CHARACTER
FLD	TRANTIME	6	29	CHARACTER
FLD	PRODGCOD	3	83	CHARACTER
LAST				VAR LEN
FLD	TRNSEGKY	19	3	CHARACTER
FLD	TRNREFNM	12	10	CHARACTER
FLD	SSABBRNM	2	20	CHARACTER
FLD	REVSFLAG	1	22	CHARACTER
FLD	TRANTIME	6	29	CHARACTER
FLD	PRODGCOD	3	83	CHARACTER
LAST				FIX LEN
FLD	CDACTNUM	11	1	CHARACTER
FLD	LBXNUMBR	4	29	CHARACTER

Data Base/Segment/Field Report for Database WCUSPAA1

DATA BASE: LP WCUSPAA1 0 TYPE: Physical
DESCRIPTION: 001 WBS Customer database
Physical database structure/ DATABASE: WCUSPAA1 STAT: L

Segment	Code	OCC	STAT	LEVL	Parent	Code	OCC	STAT	Role	DSG
CUSCUSTP	A	0	L	1					P	1
CUSSDSVP	A	0	L	2	CUSCUSTP	A	0	L	P	1
CUSCTOTP	A	0	L	3	CUSSDSVP	A	0	L		1
CUSCUTRP	A	0	L	4	CUSCTOTP	A	0	L	P	1
CUSCUACP	A	0	L	3	CUSSDSVP	A	0	L	P	1
CUSPACSP	A	0	L	4	CUSCUACP	A	0	L	P	1

SEGMENT NAME: LA CUSCUSTP 0
  SECONDARY NAME: LC CUSCUSTP 0
  Attributes effective as of 03/03/81
    LENGTH: 00300
  DESCRIPTION:
    001 WBS Same day customer segment (also WMB)

```
        01 CUSCUSTP.
              03 CUST-TRANSEND-NUM      PIC 9(4).
              03 CUST-NAME              PIC X(35).
              03 CUST-ADDR              PIC X(30).
              03 CUST-CTY               PIC X(18).
              03 CUST-ST-CNTRY          PIC X(15).
              03 CUST-ZIP-CODE          PIC X(9).
              03 CUST-PARNT-NAME        PIC X(35).
              03 CUST-CNTCT-NAME        PIC X(20).
              03 CUST-BILL-INSTRCT      PIC X(20).
              03 CUST-CONSLT-CODE       PIC XX.
              03 CUST-PSWRD             PIC X(8).
              03 TEMP-PSWRD-LAST-DT     PIC 9(6).
              03 TEMP-PSWRD-INITS       PIC X(3).
              03 CUST-BLK-FLAG          PIC X.
              03 CUST-BRDCST-FLAG       PIC X.
              03 CUST-ADD-DT            PIC 9(6).
              03 CUST-FLAG              PIC X.
              03 CUST-SVC-FLAG OCCURS   20 TIMES
                                        PIC X.
              03 CUST-SVC-TYPE-CODE     PIC XX.
              03 TEL-NUM                PIC X(15).
              03 DSCLM-CODE             PIC X.
              03 CUST-LAST-UPD-DT       PIC 9(6).
              03 DEL-FLAG               PIC X.
              03 EFF-DT                 PIC 9(6).
              03 UPD-EFF-DT             PIC 9(6).
              03 DOM-DNTRY              PIC X(5).
              03 FILLER                 PIC X(24).
```

DATA ELEMENT   : LC CUST–TRANSEND–NUM   O
  SECONDARY NAME: LA CUSTRNUM O
  DESCRIPTION:
    001 CUSTOMER–ID
    002 # TRANSEND–CUST
    003 A unique identification number assigned to a WBS/TRANSEND customer

DATA ELEMENT   : LC CUST–NAME O
  SECONDARY NAME: LA CUSTNAME O

  DESCRIPTION:
    001 CUSTOMER NAME
    002 N CUST
    003 The name of a WBS customer as it is to appear on customer reports.

DATA ELEMENT   : LC CUST–ADDR O
  SECONDARY NAME: LA CUSTADDR O

  DESCRIPTION:
    001 CUSTOMER ADDRESS
    002 A CUST
    003 The address of a customer as maintained in his profile

DATA ELEMENT   : LC CUST–CTY O
  SECONDARY NAME: LA CUSTCITY O

  DESCRIPTION:
    001 CUSTOMER CITY
    002 A CUST*CTY
    003 The city a WBS customer resides in (used for reporting purposes).

Assembler/Cobol/User Name Cross Reference for Database WACTPAA1

DATA BASE: LP WACTPAA1   O TYPE: Physical
  DESCRIPTION:
    001 ACCOUNT DATA BASE

Physical database structure/   DATABASE: WACTPAA1 STAT: L

Segment	Code	OCC	STAT	LEVL	Parent	Code	OCC	STAT	Role	DSG
ACTACCTP	A	O	L	1					P	1
ACTACCUP	A	O	L	2	ACTACCTP	A	O	L	P	1
ACTDTBLP	A	O	L	2	ACTACCTP	A	O	L	P	1
ACTPTOTP	A	O	L	3	ACTDTBLP	A	O	L	P	1
ACTCTRNP	A	O	L	3	ACTDTBLP	A	O	L	P	1
ACTDTRNP	A	O	L	3	ACTDTBLP	A	O	L	P	1
ACTCDLBP	A	O	L	2	ACTACCTP	A	O	L	P	1

Assembler/Cobol/User Name Cross Reference for Database WACTPAA1

Data Elements for Segment ACTACCTP

ASSEMBLER NAME:	ACCTNUMB	COBOL NAME:	ACCT–NUM
		USER NAME:	ACCOUNT NUMBER (WDDA)
ASSEMBLER NAME:	BCFKEYCD	COBOL NAME:	BCF–KEY
		USER NAME:	BANK CONTROL FILE KEY (BCF#)
ASSEMBLER NAME:	BCFKYLTY	COBOL NAME:	BCF–KEY–LVL–TYPE
		USER NAME:	BCF KEY LEVEL TYPE
ASSEMBLER NAME:	BCFKYLKY	COBOL NAME:	BCF–KEY–LVL–KEY
		USER NAME:	BCF KEY LEVEL KEY
ASSEMBLER NAME:	BCFKYLVL	COBOL NAME:	BCF–KEY–LVL–ID
		USER NAME:	BCF KEY LEVEL IDENTIFICATION
ASSEMBLER NAME:	DOMCTRYC	COBOL NAME:	DOM–CNTRY–CODE
		USER NAME:	COUNTRY OF DOMICILE
ASSEMBLER NAME:	AOROCODE	COBOL NAME:	AOR–CODE
		USER NAME:	AREA OF RISK OR RESPONSIBILITY
ASSEMBLER NAME:	NATLCODE	COBOL NAME:	NATLY–CODE
		USER NAME:	COUNTRY OF NATIONALITY
ASSEMBLER NAME:	SVCEAREA	COBOL NAME:	SVC–AREA
		USER NAME:	SERVICE AREA
ASSEMBLER NAME:	SDSVCARE	COBOL NAME:	SD–SVC–AREA
		USER NAME:	SAME DAY SERVICE AREA

W. D. A. System Summary Report

SUMMARY REPORT FOR SYSTEM: (K,S,TST–SUBSYSTEM–2,0)
SYS (K,S,TST-SUBSYSTEM-2,0)
  This is the second subsystem in TST–MAJOR–SYSTEM
  It has a complex structure.

Databases
  (K,P,DATABASE,0)

Transactions
  (K,,TRANS–22–1,0)
  This TRN is connected to program PGM–22–1

OS files
```
(K,,FILE-1,0)
(K,,FILE-2,0)
(K,,FIRST-FILE,0)
(K,,SECOND-FILE,0)
```
Programs
```
(K,G,PGM-1,0)
```
This is the first PGM contained in JOB-22
```
(K,G,PGM-22-1,0)
```
This is the second program in JOB 22.

Reports
```
(K,,REPORT-1,0)
(K,,REPORT-2,0)
(K,,REPORT-22-1-A,0)
```
This is the first of 2 reports produced by PGM-22-1
```
(K,,REPORT-22-1-B,0)
```

W. D. A. Program Relationships Report

PROGRAM REPORT FOR: `(K,G,PGM-22-1,0)`

```
PGM (K,G,PGM-22-1,0)
    This is the second program in JOB 22.
    Database (K,P,DATABASE,0)
    Database (K,P,DATABASE,0)
    OS-file (K,,FIRST-FILE,0)
    OS-file (K,,SECOND-FILE,0)
    Module (K,M,REUSABLE-PACKET-1,0)
    Module (K,M,REUSABLE-PACKET-2,0)
    Module (K,M,SUB-PACKET-1,0)
    Module (K,M,SUB-PACKET-2,0)
    Reports (K,,REPORT-22-1-A,0)
    Reports (K,,REPORT-22-1-B,0)
    Transactn (K,,TRANS-22-1,0)
    Program (K,G,SUB-PROGRAM-22-1,0)

      OS-file (K,,FILE,0)
      Module (K,M,SUB-MODULE-1,0)
      Module (K,M,SUB-PACKET,0)
      Reports (K,,SUB-REPORT-1,0)
      Reports (K,,SUB-REPORT-2,0)
      Transactn )K,,TRANS,0)
```
WDA0020A End of dictionary report on 10/16/81 at 17:25:50.

W. D. A. Business Function Report

SYSTEM NAME: `(K,S,TEST-REPORTS-SYSTEM,0)`
```
SYS (K,S,TEST-REPORTS-SYSTEM,0)

  BIZ_FUNC (K,,BUSINESS-FUNCTION-1,0)
```
Business function 1 description lines

```
BIZ_FUNC (K,,BUSINESS-FUNCTION-2,0)
```
Business function 2 description lines
```
BIZ_FUNC (K,,BUSINESS-FUNCTION-3,0)
```
Business function 3 description lines
This business function has no sub-functions
```
BIZ_FUNC (K,,BUSINESS-FUNCTION-4,0)
```
Business function 4 description lines
This business function has no sub-functions
But it does have two logical transactions.

WDA0020A End of dictionary report

Business Function/Transaction Report

SYSTEM NAME: (K,S,TEST-REPORTS-SYSTEM,0)

```
SYS (K,S,TEST-REPORTS-SYSTEM,0)
  BIZ_FUNC (K,,BUSINESS-FUNCTION-1,0)
```
   Business function 1 description lines
```
  BIZ_FUNC (K,,BUSINESS-FUNCTION-2,0)
```
   Business function 2 description lines
```
  BIZ_FUNC (K,,BUSINESS-FUNCTION-3,0)
```
   Business function 3 description lines
   This business function has no sub-functions
```
  LOG_TRAN (K,,LOGICAL-TRANSACTION-8,0)
```
   Description lines for logical transaction 8
   A clear concise definition of the logical transaction
```
  BIZ_Func (K,,BUSINESS-FUNCTION-4,0)
```
   Business function 4 description lines
   This business function has no sub-functions
   But it does have two logical transactions
```
  LOG_TRAN (K,,LOGICAL-TRANSACTION-9,0)
```
   Description lines for logical transaction 9
```
  LOG_TRAN (K,,LOGICAL-TRANSACTION-10,0)
```
   Description lines for logical transaction 10

WDA0020A End of dictionary report

Case History 2

1. Introduction

In response to your request, we have two dictionaries currently in use:
- UCCTEN which is used for our IMS DN/DC systems
- PREDICT which is used for our ADABAS/NATURAL systems

2. Metadata

UCCTEN

(a) *Name of Field.* The field name in UCCTEN is restricted to eight characters (A-Z, 0-9, special characters, no blanks), and is used to accurately describe the field itself, without relating it to its intended function.

(b) *Alias.* Alias (synonyms) are defined as a new definition of an existing field. An alias is a field with the same name but with different physical characteristics i.e., picture, type, justification, usage. A maximum of 256 alias' may be defined.

(c) *Actual Description.* Textual information may be added to the field in three separate areas: general description, edit description, and source/responsibility.

(d) *Function.* The function of a field is defined in the textual information associated with that field.

(e) *Acceptance Status.* A field is accepted once it has been approved. Field data may be changed, provided that policies, procedures, and standards are followed. The actual physical changes are the responsibility of the Data Dictionary Administrator.

(f) *Definition Responsibility.* The Data Dictionary Administrator is responsible for the contents of the dictionary. However, the project team has the ultimate responsibility for ensuring the data's accuracy and integrity.

(g) *Access Authority.* All users have inquiry access against fields, but only the Data Dictionary Administrator may update a field.

(h) *Validity and Edit Rules.* Validity and edit rules for a field are stored as part of the edit text. However, these rules must be incorporated into programs as the dictionary does not perform any validity checks.

(i) *Consistency Checks (Ranges).* See above.

(j) *Reasonableness Checks.* See above.

(k) *Usage Propagation.* Reports are available through UCCTEN which provide information on where the field is used and by whom.

(l) *Validation Propagation.* Reports are available through UCCTEN which provide information on what impact a change will make; i.e., who, what, where, when and how.

PREDICT

(a) *Name of Field.* The name assigned to a field in PREDICT must be at least three but not more than 32 characters in length. The first character must be alpabetic (A-Z). All other characters must be alphanumeric (A-Z, 0-9), the hyphen or a blank). The field name itself must consist of three components connected by hyphens (no blanks allowed):

- Entity keyword
- Descriptive keyword(s)
- Class keyword

Where

1. An entity keyword is a person, place, thing or event about which data is required.

2. A descriptive keyword further describes the data.

3. A class keyword identifies the general type of use of the data (e.g., NUN, NAME, QTY, FLAG).

(b) *Alias.* Alias' (synonyms) are alternate field names that can be assigned to a data element for use by Natural, COBOL, PL/1 and Assembler. Up to nine different synonyms may be specified per language. However, if a synonym is assigned the original data element name may not be referenced.

(c) *Actual Description.* Each data element may contain both user and an edit description which provide additional information.

(d) *Function.* The function of a field is defined in the user comments and/or edit description associated with that field.

(e) *Acceptance Status.* A field is accepted once it has been approved. Field data may be changed, provided that policies, procedures, and standards are followed. The actual physical changes are the responsibility of the Data Dictionary Administrator.

(f) *Definition Responsibility.* The Data Dictionary Administrator is responsible for the contents of the dictionary. However, the project team has the ultimate responsibility for ensuring the data's accuracy and integrity.

(g) *Access Authority.* Currently, no one but the Data Administration group has access to PREDICT due to the fact that security levels may not be applied. However, all users may browse hard copy printouts.

(h) *Validity and Edit Rules.* The verification object names and describes a field verification procedure. The verification entry may describe the type of verification, whether it be a range of values, equal to, less than, greater than, a user or a table. Values to be used to perform the verification may also be identified. However, the verification information as stored on the dictionary is used for documentation purposes only. No attempt is made to verify actual data values against verification data contained in the dictionary.

(i) *Consistency Checks (Ranges).* See above.

(j) *Reasonableness Checks.* See above.

(k) *Usage Propagation.* PREDICT offers a comprehensive set of dictionary information retrieval functions, in both online and batch mode, which can be used to determine where the field is used and by whom.

(l) *Validation Propagation.* A major advantage of PREDICT is the ability to "predict" the impact of proposed changes on a global scale, i.e. to perform an impact analysis of how many users, reports, programs, etc, would be affected by a proposed or required data structure or data content modification or enhancement. This capability permits a more rational approach to the planning of modifications which may have a significant impact on the current information system environment.

3. Contents

UCCTEN

UCCTEN is a central source of data base definitions, program definitions, communication system definitions, format descriptors, message descriptors, documentation and Application Development Facility (ADF) definitions.

PREDICT

PREDICT contains information about an organization's data and its use. Data entries in the dictionary describe the data base, files, fields, verification procedures, and relationships between files. Any data (not only the ADABAS data base) may be described in the dictionary entries. Usage entries in the dictionary are of two types; personnel and processing. Personnel entries describe the owners and users of data and processing entries. Processing entries describe systems, programs, modules and reports. All entires contain maintenance information.

4. Role of data dictionary

UCCTEN

UCCTEN provides the capability to define and describe Data Base/Data Communication systems (DL/I IMS), or any other application system (non-IMS) using any standard OS file organization. Provisions are included in UCCTEN for automated documentation assistance, centralized data field definitions and programmer coding aids.

UCCTEN is a passive dictionary used to store all IMS and non-IMS physical structures (including screen definitions) and data element definitions.

PREDICT

PREDICT is an online semi-active data dictionary facility which provides an organization with the capability of creating and maintaining current dictionary data in an online environment. The following types of dictionary information may be stored and maintained in PREDICT.

- Information about the organization's processing environment
- Information about the data, personnel, processing entities, and the relationship between them

5. Maintenance of Data Dictionary

UCCTEN

Processing can occur in UCCTEN in either online or batch modes, or transactions may be entered through an online terminal for later batch processing.

Formal procedures are in place which must be adhered to. Forms are provided for the Project Teams to define the data elements required. The data element forms are then approved by the Data Dictionary Administrator and keyed in by a clerical resource. All other data structures are created by the Data Base Analyst, with the exception of screens (message/format structures) which are designed and input by the Project Team.

PREDICT

Dictionary information may be added using input screens for each type of dictionary object. In addition, information from an existing ADABAS file definition or a Data Definition Module (DDM) may be used as input for the creation of dictionary information.

Formal procedures are in place which must be adhered to. Forms are provided for the Data Modelling Analysts to define the data elements required. The data element forms are then approved by the Data Dictionary Administrator and keyed in by a clerical resource. All other data structures are created by the Data Base Analysts.

6. Control and Audit Features

UCCTEN

UCCTEN is designed to assist Data Base Administration in establishing and maintaining control of the data base environment for IMS DL/I and non-IMS data bases. Although this control is used to assist the Data Base Administrator, it becomes apparent that UCCTEN is designed to assist application programmers, system programmers, operators and management in the performance of their duties as well.

Additionally, relationship information between the different elements in UCCTEN allows the control function to answer such questions as: What programs can access a given segment? What segments does this program access? What programs access this data base or file?

IMS helps to protect UCCTEN and ensure data integrity by maintaining a complete audit trail of the activity against the data base on the IMS log tape.

PREDICT

PREDICT is designed to assist Data Base Administration in establishing and maintaining control of the data base environment for ADABAS and non-ADABAS files.

Cross reference information between the different objects in PREDICT allows the control function to answer a question such as: What files, relationships, modules, reports, programs and/or systems is this field included in?

ADABAS helps to protect PREDICT and ensure data integrity by maintaining a complete audit trail of the activity against the data base on the ADABAS data protection log.

7. Standards

UCCTEN

UCCTEN provides the ability to enforce standard naming conventions through user-written edit routines. Such user exits have been used to control a comprehensive set of naming conventions. The exits also manage all security for the dictionary; i.e., the presence or absence of passwords on transactions allow or disallow certain functions to be performed.

PREDICT

PREDICT does not provide the ability to enforce standard naming conventions as there are no user exits nor is the source code available. Therefore, limited access is provided to PREDICT which relieves it of its "user-friendly" qualities. PREDICT however, does support ADABAS security which may be applied at the file, field and value level. This method of securing ADABAS can become quite complex though, and becomes easier to manage if combined with NATURAL Security.

8. Data Dictionary as a Tool for Data Analysis

UCCTEN

The facility does exist in UCCTEN, whereby entities and relationships can be defined by using the current established structures. Keyword in context information also provides search capabilities for existing definitions on keyword or partial keywords.

PREDICT

PREDICT allows for the creation and maintenance of the logical data model, which can be stored separately from the physical structure. As well, data relationships are supported. Automatic coupling between entities within files is also available. Coupling between files can also be done either dynamically or by pre-definition.

A

Entity Class Definition Contents

1.1 Definition Subject

An *entity class definition* is a category of entry in the definition library describing a particular view of entities which exist in the external world.

An *entity* is defined to be any object, real or imaginary, which can be thought of as having a distinct and identifiable existence. Entities are the objects which underlay all corporate functions. The data collected and processed within the organization represents the information about those objects relevant to company operations and business methods.

Entities can be described in terms of their attributes. Different views of the same entity can be obtained by selecting different attributes of that entity. For example, consider a person who works for a company. By some groups in the company, that person is viewed as an employee. By other groups, the same person is viewed as a customer to whom the company provides telephone service. For each view a discrete set of attributes can be identified reflecting the information needs of the different departments.

In the definition library, these distinct views are designated "entity classes." An *entity class* is defined as a collection of attributes which provide a complete description of an entity in a particular role. Thus a person entity in the role of an employee gives rise to the entity class "employee," while in that same person in the role of a customer gives rise to the entity class "customer."

The objective of data modeling is to identify the complete set of attributes which make up an entity class. Once an entity class is established, it can be viewed as the formal definition of a conceptual object which exists in its own right and interacts with other conceptual objects through well-defined entity relationships. It is this association between entity classes and conceptual objects which results in references to employee entities and customer entities rather than the real objects (i.e., the people) on which those entity classes are based.

Entity classes are not static. Because they are based upon the business practices used in the company and because those business practices change with time, entity classes evolve. It is essential that all physical data structures defined to be representations of an entity class have similar capability.

1.2   Definition Contents

The components of an entity class definition include:

- The primary name and aliases used to reference the entity class and to identify its role within the organization
- General descriptive information about the entity class and its members
- Symbolic references used to locate the entity class definition within the definition library
- The names of project teams and organizational groups with an ongoing interest in the definition and its updates
- The names of organizational groups responsible for the ongoing accuracy and integrity of the definition
- The names of attributes which make up the entity class

1.3   Definition Components

The following pages describe the fields and sections which make up an entity class definition.

Library entry identifier.   An 8-character alphanumeric identifier assigned to individual entries in the definition library.

This identifier takes the form XXXNNNNN, where XXX is a 3-character alphabetic field identifying the library volume containing the definition and NNNNN is a 5-character numeric field which uniquely identifies the entry within the volume.

Entity class name.   A symbolic or descriptive name conventionally used to identify the entity class and the type of objects it represents.

An entity class name consists of from 1 to 50 characters constructed from the following character set:

- Uppercase alphabetic characters.
- Numeric characters.
- The special symbols hyphen, comma, slash, period, and blank. The

```
             EXHIBIT: COMPONENTS OF AN ENTITY CLASS DEFINITION

a) External parameters
     <library entry identifier>
b) Internal sections
     = = NAME: <entity class name>
     = = ALIASES
     <alias name 1> (<context or usage comments>)
     .............................................
     <alias name n> (<context or usage comments>)
     = = CLASSIFICATION
         ENTITY CLASS DEFINITION
     = = DESCRIPTION
         <entity class description>
     = = FUNCTION
         1. <entity class function 1>
         ............................
         n. <entity class function n>
     = = DEFINITION UPDATE SOURCE
         <source 1>  (<date 1>)
         ....................
         <source n>  (<date n>)
     = = USER ACCEPTANCE STATUS
         <status code 1>  (<group 1>)
         ...........................
         <status code n>, <group n>
     = = DEFINITION RESPONSIBILITY
         <position title 1>
         ..................
         <position title n>
     = = ATTRIBUTES
         <attribute name 1>
         ..................
         <attribute name n>
```

special symbols are used to format the name. For indexing and cross-referencing purposes, they are treated as blanks.

An entity class name is terminated by the following:

- The last alphabetic or numeric character immediately preceding the left most bracket symbol (.

All characters to the right of and including the bracket symbol (are treated as blanks. Comments and qualifications, enclosed by the bracket symbols (and) can be freely appended to an entity class name but cannot be embedded in the name.

All names longer than 50 characters must be truncated, or their length reduced to 50 characters or less using standard abbreviations. When abbreviations are used, the full name should be explicitly stated in the entity class description.

Entity class names must be selected within the guidelines listed below.

1. The name should be unique within the definition library. The data library support software can handle homonyms, but the onus is on the library user to ensure that attribute references resolve to the correct definition.

2. The name must take one of the following forms:

   AAAA   A descriptive name with no embedded commas. This can be used for any entity class. A typical example would be the name "position."

   EEEE,SSSS   A composite name used for entity classes representing subgroups of some larger and more general entity class. EEEE denotes the entity class name of the more general class, and SSSS represents the qualifier identifying the subclass. An example would be "invoice, local purchase order" denoting an invoice received for goods obtained on a local purchase order.

3. The name should be concise but sufficiently descriptive that a user can gain a general appreciation of the objects which make up the entity class without reference to the full entity class definition.

4. The name should be independent of any single application system, reflecting the fact that entity class should identify objects of interest to the corporation as a whole.

5. Abbreviations within the name should be limited to situations in which the full name would exceed the maximum allowable length for an entity class name.

The specific representation of the entity class name section is as follows:

```
= = NAME: <dictionary entry name>
= = <title of next section>
```

Aliases. A list of names used as alternate identifiers for the entity class and its representations.

Each name consists of from 1 to 50 characters constructed from the following character set:

- Uppercase alphabetic characters.

- Numeric characters.

- The special symbols hyphen, commas, slash, period, and blank. The special symbols are used to format the name. For indexing and cross-referencing purposes, they are treated as blanks.

Names designated as aliases are terminated by any of the following:

- The last alphabetic or numeric character immediately preceding the leftmost bracket symbol (.
- The last alphabetic or numeric character in positions 1 to 50, inclusive, if the name contains no bracket symbol (

All characters to the right of and including the bracket symbol (are treated as blanks. Comments enclosed in brackets can be freely appended to an alias name but they cannot be embedded in the name.

Alias names provide a set of alternate identifiers for referencing entity class definitions and entity class representations. By appending comments to the names in the list, the primary usage of the alias name can be identified.

The standard format for the section is as follows:

```
= = ALIASES
    <alias name 1> (<context or usage comments>)
    . . . . . . . . . . . . . . . . . . . . . . . . . . . . . . . . . . . . . . . . . .
    <alias name n> (<context or usage comments>)
= = <title of next section>
```

Library entry classification. A descriptive code assigned to all library entries, identifying the type of definition.

For an entity class definition, the classification code takes the value "entity class definition" and is documented as follows:

```
= = CLASSIFICATION
    ENTITY CLASS DEFINITION
= = <title of next section>
```

Entity class description. A freeform narrative containing a description of the entity class and the objects on which it is based.

The description contains

1. A concise definition of the entity class in a form suitable for use in a glossary. This definition occupies the first paragraph of the section and, ideally, should be 4 lines or less in length. When abbreviations are used in the entity class name, the full name should be included in the opening sentence.

2. A brief description of the objects, real or imaginary, which serve as the basis for the entity class.

3. A summary of the attributes and entity relationships associated with objects assigned to the entity class.

4. A description of the criteria used to add new members to the set of objects which compose the entity class, and the criteria for their subsequent deletion.

5. A set of references to the major representations of the entity class. This may include

- IMS databases
- Mechanized files
- Clerical files

The description section is documented as follows:

```
= = DESCRIPTION
      <entity class description>
= = <title of next section>
```

Entity class function.   A freeform narrative describing the corporate interest in the entity class and its physical representations.
   The narrative describes

1. The purpose and usage of the entity class as it relates to corporate objectives and the business functions used to achieve them
2. The local purpose served by the entity class in application systems
3. The intended future use of the entity class where that differs from its current role

Occurrences of entity class function are optional and are usually restricted to entity classes in which the intended usage is obscure, or where it is appropriate to stress their role in company operations. When the function is documented, the following format is used:

```
= = FUNCTION
      1. <entity class function 1>
      . . . . . . . . . . . . . . . . . . . . . . . . . .
      n. <entity class function n>
= = <title of next section>
```

Definition update source.   A composite structure identifying the individuals or groups who have updated a library entry and the dates on which those updates were made.
   A single occurrence of the structure is recorded for each update. It takes the form:

```
<source> (<date>)
```

<source> is a 3-character field identifying the person or group who submitted the definition modification. Values of this field are conventionally derived from the initials of the person or group who first documented the definition or who subsequently submitted an update. The subfield <date> is a 6-digit date field in the format YYMMDD

representing the date on which definition was created or modified. By convention, values of this field normally reflect the date on which the changes were keyed into the definition library.

The specific representation of update information takes the form:

```
= = DEFINITION UPDATE SOURCE
    <source 1> (<date 1>)
    .....................
    <source n> (<date n>)
= = <title of next section>
```

User acceptance status.   A composite structure identifying the project teams or organizational groups who created the definition or who must be informed of its subsequent updates.

The structure is used

1. As the basis for propagating definition changes to support groups who may be affected by the proposed modifications
2. To control the evolution of definition library entries from their initial form to the final versions accepted on a corporate basis.

A single occurrence of the structure is recorded for each group. It takes the form

```
<status code>, <group name>
```

<status code> is a 1-character code representing the degree of acceptance of the library entry relative to the group identified by <group name>. It can take the following values:

Code	Meaning
I	The library entry represents a preliminary definition proposed by the associated systems-development group. The definition may be changed at will by the team with no consultation with other users.
P	The library entry represents a working definition created or modified by the associated group. The definition may be changed, but only after consultation with all users indicating an acceptance code of P or A.
A	The library entry in its current form has been accepted as a working definition by the associated group. Changes in the definition can only be made after consultation with that group.
C	The library entry in its current form is ready for final review and acceptance by the group charged with responsibility for its ongoing integrity.
E	The library entry has been accepted by the groups assigned definition responsibility. Any further changes must be explicitly approved by those groups.

Status codes C and E are restricted to use in corporate library volumes. Status codes P and A can appear in any library volumes, while status code I is restricted to project library volumes.

User acceptance status information is assigned by data administration, on request and after consultation with the groups affected by a proposed status change. For definitions in a project library volume, if no status information exists, the definition is assumed to have status code I for the group to which the library volume belongs.

The specific representation of acceptance status information takes the form

```
= = USER ACCEPTANCE STATUS
      <status code 1>, <group 1>
      ............................
      <status code n>, <group n>
= = <title of next section>
```

Definition responsibility. A set of references to the organizational groups charged with the responsibility for the accuracy and ongoing integrity of a definition.

References consist of a maximum of 50 characters derived from the position titles of the organizational groups. These position titles are obtained from the organization charts maintained by the personnel department.

Definition responsibility references are used to establish a relationship between a library entry and the organizational groups identified as the definitive source of information about the entity class meaning and use. No changes can be made in a library entry after its acceptance by these groups, without their prior approval.

The standard representation for definition responsibility information is

```
= = DEFINITION RESPONSIBILITY
      <position title 1>
      .................
      <position title n>
= = <title of next section>
```

Entity class attributes. A list of names identifying the attributes which are associated with the entity class.

The names in the list must correspond to the names associated with entity class definitions recorded elsewhere in the definition library.

The standard format for the section is

```
= = ATTRIBUTES
      <attribute name 1>
      .................
      <attribute name n>
```

Logical Group Definition Contents

1.1 Definition Subject

A *logical group definition* is a category of entry in the definition LIBRARY describing a set of attributes grouped together on the basis of common usage, access requirements, or source.

Logical groups are implementation-oriented groups of attributes, gathered together to simplify the collection of data-usage statistics and the design of the physical database.

Each logical group is assigned to a specific entity class, and in combination with other similar groups it can be viewed as a specific representation of that entity class. For logical groups containing entity attributes only, the entity class is the class to which the attributes belong. For logical groups representing a relationship between two entities, the logical group implies a unidirectional association between the source entity class (the class to which the group belongs) and the target entity class (the class to which at least part of the group contents must point).

Logical groups consist of

- Attributes which represent an explicit relationship between two entity classes. An example might be the group of attributes which describe the "position assignment" relationship between an employee and a position.

- Attributes which represent an implicit relationship between an identified entity class and an abstract entity not formally defined within the definition library. An example would be the group of attributes describing an employee's participation or status in the pension plan.

- Attributes which share a common functional basis and occur with the same frequencies. An example might be the set of address attributes held for an employee.
- Attributes which share the same data security or privacy requirements.

The composition of a logical group is subjective. The precise relationship between an attribute and an entity or entity relationship exists independently of the assignment of that attribute to a particular logical group. Nevertheless, because logical groups figure prominently in the database-design process, care must be exercised in defining their contents to minimize the need for major database restructuring.

1.2 Definition contents

The components of a logical group definition include

- The primary name and aliases used to reference the logical group
- General descriptive information identifying the criteria underlying the logical group contents
- Symbolic references used to locate the logical group definition within the definition library
- The names of project teams and organizational groups with an ongoing interest in the definition and its updates
- The names of organizational groups responsible for the ongoing accuracy and integrity of the definition
- The names of the logical schemas with which the logical group is associated
- The names of attributes which make up the logical group
- References to other entries in the definition library associated in some specific manner with the logical group
- The names of the IMS segments with which the logical group is associated

1.3 Definition Components

The fields and sections which make up a logical group definition are described below.

Library entry identifier. An 8-character alphanumeric identifier assigned to individual entries in the definition library.

```
                   EXHIBIT: Contents of a Logical Group Definition
a)  External parameters
        <library entry identifier>
b)  Internal sections
    = = NAME: <logical group name>
    = = ALIASES
        <alias name 1> (<context or usage comments>)
        . . . . . . . . . . . . . . . . . . . . . . . . . . . . . . .
        <alias name n> (<context or usage comments>)
    = = CLASSIFICATION
        LOGICAL GROUP DEFINITION
    = = DESCRIPTION
        <logical group description>
    = = DEFINITION UPDATE SOURCE
        <source 1> (<date 1>)
        . . . . . . . . . . . . . . . . . . .
        <source n> (<date n>)
    = =USER ACCEPTANCE STATUS
        <status code 1>, <group 1>
        . . . . . . . . . . . . . . . . . . . . . . . . .
        <status code n>, <group n>
    = =DEFINITION RESPONSIBILITY
        <position title 1>
        . . . . . . . . . . . . . . . . .
        <position title n>
    = =MEMBERSHIP
        <logical schema name 1>
        . . . . . . . . . . . . . . . . . . . . . .
        <logical schema name n>
    = = CONTENTS
           <logical group name>
        XXXX <indented attribute name 1>
        . . . . . . . . . . . . . . . . . . . . . . . . . . . . . . .
        XXXX <indented attribute name 1>
    = =REPRESENTATIONS
        <language 1>-<member name 1> <library name 1>
        . . . . . . . . . . . . . . . . . . . . . . . . . . . . . . . . . . . . . .
        <language n>-<member name n> <library name n>
    = =IMS SEGMENT REPRESENTATION
        <IMS segment name 1>
        . . . . . . . . . . . . . . . . . . .
        <IMS segment name n>
```

This identifier takes the form XXXNNNNN, where XXX is a 3-character alphabetic field identifying the library volume containing the definition and NNNNN is a 5-character numeric field which serves as a unique identifier within a volume.

Logical group name. A symbolic or descriptive name conventionally used to identify the logical group and its representations.

A logical group name consists of from 1 to 50 characters constructed from the following character set:

- Uppercase alphabetic characters.
- Numeric characters.
- The special symbols hyphen, slash, and blank. The special symbols are used to format the name. For indexing and cross-referencing purposes, they are treated as blanks.

A logical group name is terminated by any of the following:

- The last alphabetic or numeric character immediately preceding the leftmost bracket symbol (
- The last alphabetic or numeric character in positions 1 to 50 inclusive if the name contains no bracket symbol (

All characters to the right of and including the bracket symbol (are treated as blanks. Comments and qualifications, enclosed by the bracket symbols (and), can be freely appended to a logical group name but cannot be embedded in the name.

All names longer than 50 characters must be truncated, or their length reduced to 50 characters or less, using standard abbreviations. When abbreviations are used, the full name should be explicitly stated in the logical group description.

Logical group names must be selected within the guidelines below.

1. The name must be unique within the definition library.
2. The name must take the following form:
   AAAA   A descriptive name with no embedded commas. A typical example would be the name EMPLOYEE UNION STATUS GROUP.
3. The name should be concise but sufficiently descriptive that a user can gain a general appreciation of its source or contents without reference to the full definition.
4. Abbreviations within the name should be limited to situations in which the full name would exceed the maximum allowable length for a logical group name.

The specific representation of the logical group name section is as follows:

```
= = NAME: <dictionary entry name>
= = <title of next section>
```

Aliases. A list of names used as alternate identifiers for the logical group.

Each name consists of from 1 to 50 characters constructed from the following character set:

- Uppercase alphabetic characters.
- Numeric characters.
- The special symbols hyphen, comma, slash, period, and blank. The special symbols are used to format the name. For indexing and cross-referencing purposes, they are treated as blanks.

Names designated as aliases are terminated by any of the following:

- The last alphabetic or numeric character immediately preceding the leftmost bracket symbol (
- The last alphabetic or numeric character in positions 1 to 50 inclusive if the name contains no bracket symbol (

All characters to the right of and including the bracket symbol (are treated as blanks. Comments enclosed in brackets can be freely appended to an alias name but cannot be embedded in the name.

Alias names provide a set of alternate identifiers for referencing logical group definitions and logical group representations. By appending comments to the names in the list, the primary usage of the alias name can be identified.

The standard format for the section is as follows:

```
= = ALIASES
    <alias name 1> (<context or usage comments>)
    ...........................................
    <alias name n> (<context or usage comments>)
= = <title of next section>
```

Library entry classification.   A descriptive code assigned to all library entries, identifying the type of definition.

For a logical group definition, the classification code takes the value LOGICAL GROUP DEFINITION and is documented as follows:

```
= = CLASSIFICATION
    LOGICAL GROUP DEFINITION
= = <title of next section>
```

Logical group description.   A freeform narrative containing a description of the logical group.

The description contains

1. A concise definition of the logical group in a form suitable for use within a user glossary or similar document. This definition occupies the first paragraph of the section and, ideally, should be 4 lines or less in length. When abbreviations are used in the formal logical group name, the full unabbreviated name should be included in the opening sentence.

2. An overview of the attributes which make up the logical group with particular reference to any internal structure.

3. A statement of the criteria used in the formation of the logical group. These are documented in order to allow future changes to the logical group to be assessed relative to the initial criteria.

Definition update source.   A composite structure identifying the individuals or groups who have updated a library entry and the dates on which those updates were made.

A single occurrence of the structure is recorded for each update. It takes the form

```
<source> (<date>)
```

<source> is a 3-character field identifying the person or group who submitted the definition modification. Values of this field are conventionally derived from the initials of the person or group who first documented the definition or who subsequently submitted an update. The subfield <date> is a 6-digit date field in the format YYMMDD representing the date on which the definition was created or modified. By convention, values of this field normally reflect the date on which the changes were keyed into the definition library.

The specific representation of update information takes the form

```
= = DEFINITION UPDATE SOURCE
  <source 1> (<date 1>)
  ....................
  <source n> (<date n>)
```

User acceptance status.   A composite structure identifying the project teams or organizational groups who created the definition or who must be informed of its subsequent updates.

The structure is used

1. As the basis for propagating definition changes to support groups who may be affected by the proposed modifications

2. To control the evolution of definition library entries from their initial form to the final versions accepted on a corporate basis

A single occurrence of the structure is recorded for each group. It takes the form

```
<status code>, <group name>
```

<status code> is a 1-character code representing the degree of acceptance of the library entry relative to the group identified by <group name>. It can take the following values:

Code	Meaning
I	The library entry represents a preliminary definition proposed by the associated systems development group. The definition may be changed at will by the team with no consultation with other users.
P	The library entry represents a working definition created or modified by the associated group. The definition may be changed, but only after consultation with all users indicating an acceptance code of P or A.
A	The library entry in its current form has been accepted as a working definition by the associated group. Changes in the definition can only be made after consultation with that group.
C	The library entry in its current form is ready for final review and acceptance by the group charged with responsibility for its ongoing integrity.
E	The library entry has been accepted by the groups assigned definition responsibility. Any further changes must be explicitly approved by those groups.

Status codes C and E are restricted to use in corporate library volumes. Status codes P and A can appear in any library volumes, while status code I is restricted to project library volumes.

User acceptance status information is assigned by data administration, on request, and after consultation with the groups affected by a proposed status change. For definitions in a project library volume, if no status information exists, the definition is assumed to have status code I for the group to which the library volume belongs.

The specific representation of acceptance status information takes the form

```
= = USER ACCEPTANCE STATUS
      <status code 1>, <group 1>
      ..........................
      <status code n>, <group n>
= = <title of next section>
```

Definition responsibility. A set of references to the organizational groups charged with the responsibility for the accuracy and ongoing integrity of a definition.

References consist of a maximum of 50 characters derived from the position titles of the organizational groups. These position titles are obtained from the organization charts maintained by the personnel department.

Definition responsibility references are used to establish a relationship between a library entry and the organizational groups identified as the definitive source of information about the logical group's meaning and use. No changes can be made in a library entry after its acceptance by these groups, without their prior approval.

The standard representation for definition responsibility information is

```
= = DEFINITION RESPONSIBILITY
    <position title 1>
    . . . . . . . . . . . . . . . . .
    <position title n>
= = <title of next section>
```

Logical schema membership. A list of names identifying the logical schemas containing occurrences of the logical group.

The names in the list must correspond to the names associated with logical schema definitions stored elsewhere in the definition library.

The standard format for the section is as follows:

```
= = MEMBERSHIP
    <logical schema name 1>
    . . . . . . . . . . . . . . . . . . . . .
    <logical schema name n>
= = <title of next section>
```

Logical Group Contents. A collection of attribute names, arranged in hierarchial notation, identifying the components of the logical group and their internal relationships.

The section is documented as shown below.

1. *Basic notation.*
    ```
    <logical group name>
    ```
    XXXX <component name 1, indented to appropriate level>
    XXXX <component name n, indented to appropriate level>
    The logical group name always occupies the first line of the section and serves as the anchor point for indenting subsequent group component names. Each level of indentation represents 1 level in the group component hierarchy. Dependencies between components

are reflected by relative differences in their indentations. For example, if B1, B2, and B3 in logical group PQR are dependent upon A1 and if C1 is dependent upon B2, then group PQR is described as follows:

```
        PQR
XXXX    A1
XXXX      B1
XXXX      B2
XXXX        C1
XXXX      B3
```

Note that B1, B2, and B3 are indented by the same amount relative to A1 and that C1 is indented with respect to B2. In addition, for consistency, A1 is indented 1 level with respect to PQR, signifying it is the highest-level component of the group.

Field XXXX denotes a relationship description value describing the association between a group component and its parent 1 level higher in the hierarchy. In the example, the value of XXXX for C1 describes its relationship to B2. The values of XXXX for B1, B2, and B3, in turn, describe the associations between those components and component A1.

For logical groups, XXXX can take the following values:

XXXX	Interpretation
OOAA	For each occurrence of the parent there must be one and only one occurrence of the dependent.
OOSA	For each occurrence of the parent there may be zero occurrences or a single occurrence of the dependent.
OMAA	For each occurrence of the parent there must be at least one occurrence of the dependent, and there may be many.
OMSA	For each occurrence of the parent there may be any number of occurrences of the dependent, including zero.

For the parent-dependent relationship B2–C1 in the example above, the values of XXXX for C1 are interpreted as follows:

XXXX	B1 occurrences	C1 occurrences
OOAA	1	1
OOSA	1	0,1
OMAA	1	$1, 2 \ldots n$
OMSA	1	$0, 1 \ldots n$

2. *Treatment of multilevel dependencies.* Dependencies between group components are represented by indentation. For direct relationships between two components, single-level indentation is used. For example,

```
. . . G1
OMSA H1
```

The example indicates the occurrences of H1 are dependent upon occurrences of G1.

For dependencies involving three or more components, multilevel indentation must be used. If Z1 depends on both Y1 and X1, then the dependency can be expressed in two forms:

```
. . . . . X1          or    . . . . .  Y1
    OMSA       Y1              OMSA         X1
    OOAA       Z1              OOAA         Z1
```

The first structure means that for an occurrence of X1 there can be many occurrences of Y1, and for each occurrence of Y1 there must always be an occurrence of Z1. The second structure has the roles of Y1 and X1 interchanged. The choice of form depends upon whether X1 or Y1 is viewed as the major key. The left form considers X1 the major key; the right form places Y1 in that role.

This nesting of levels can proceed to any depth, although experience suggests that anything more than 4 levels should be treated with caution.

3. *Treatment of subgroups.* It is a common requirement to identify and treat a subgrouping of components as a higher-level component in its own right. This sub-grouping is documented as follows:

```
. . . . A1
OMAA  (subgroup XYZ)
OOAA  B1
OOAA  D1
OMSA  E1
```

(Subgroup XYZ) identifies a subgroup which contains one occurrence of B1 and one of D1. The subgroup as a whole is defined to be a dependent of A1, and the relationship specification OMAA indicates there must always be at least one occurrence of that subgroup for each occurrence of A1. Each component of the subgroup must be indented at least 1 level with respect to the subgroup name, and deeper nesting may exist if the subgroup itself contains internal dependencies. The first group component at the same level or a higher level than the subgroup name terminates the subgroup and is not considered a subgroup component. In the example, subgroup XYZ is terminated by E1, but although E1 is a dependent of A1 it is not a component of XYZ.

In effect, subgroups can be considered single components at all higher levels. They are particularly useful for documenting repeating groups or sets of group components which are considered indivisible.

4. *Mutually exclusive group components.* Occasionally, a group structure references mutually exclusive components. Either one component must be present or the other, but not both. This is expressed as follows:

```
. . . . A1
 OOAA  B1
 -OR-   C1
```

A1 has dependents B1 and C1 which are mutually exclusive. For each occurrence of A1 there must be an occurrence of B1 or an occurrence of C1 but not both. This association between B1 and C1 is represented by the –OR– symbol which takes the place of the usual relationship description. The association OOAA associated with B1 applies to the total set of components linked by the –OR– symbol.

More complicated structures can be produced by linking together subgroups and individual group components. As an example,

```
 .  .  .  .  A1
 OOAA       B1
 -OR-       (subgroup PQR)
 OOAA       P1
 -OR-         Q1
 -OR-       (subgroup XYZ)
 OMSA         X1
```

An occurrence of A1 has as its dependents one and only one occurrence of either B1 or (subgroup PQR) or (subgroup XYZ). PQR consists of an occurrence of P1 or an occurrence of Q1. XYZ consists of many occurrences of X1.

5. *Treatment of comments.* General comments can be freely added to the group contents. They can take one of two forms:

```
. . . . P1
 OOAA  Q1  (this is the first comment type)
 OMSA  R1
          This is the second type of comment
 OMSA  S1
```

The first form consists of bracketed text appended to a group component name. It is used to qualify the group component name or to provide additional descriptive information.

The second form consists of unbracketed text on a line with a blank relationship description field. This form can be used anywhere within the section, and blank lines are acceptable. It is used for footnotes or explanatory text, or to improve the presentation of the group structure.

6. *Unresolved relationship descriptions.* Throughout the earlier subsections, specific values of the relationship description field XXXXX have been introduced to serve various needs. If a suitable value can not be assigned or if the value is irrelevant, two options are open. The first option is to leave the field blank, i.e., to treat each group component name as a comment. Group structure can be expressed by identation, but this method has the disadvantage that many of the mechanized cross-reference facilities, particularly error and warning diagnostics, will not be fully effective.

The second and recommended option is to set the field value to four hyphens, ----. This identifies the associated text as a group component name and supports the full cross-reference and diagnostic facilities.

The standard representation of the section is as follows:

```
= = CONTENTS
     <logical group name>
     XXXX <indented group component name 1>
     . . . . . . . . . . . . . . . . . . . . . . . . . . . . . . . . . . .
     XXXX <indented group component name n>
= = <title of next section
```

Note: The relationship description values used for logical groups are a subset of the values which can be used to describe a relationship between any two objects.

Representations. A set of references to source code library members whose contents describe the logical group structure in a particular programming language.

A single reference takes the form

```
<language>-<member name><library identifier>
```

<language> identifies the target programming subsystem for the library contents. It can take the values

```
COBOL
MARKIV
ADF
```

<member name> identifies the name of the source library member. It consists of from 1 to 8 characters satisfying the naming rules for members in a partitioned data set.

<library identifier> identifies the library, either by data set name or by some suitable mnemonic. The combination of <member name> and <library name> must provide a unique identifier for individual source code modules.

The standard format for the section is as follows:

```
= = REPRESENTATIONS
     <language 1>-<member name 1><library name 1>
     .........................................
     <language n>-<member name n><library name n>
= = <title of next section>
```

IMS segment representation. A list of names identifying the IMS segment types derived from the logical group. The names adhere to the convention outlined in the IMS segment type definition for naming segments.

The standard representation of the section is as follows:

```
= = IMS SEGMENT REPRESENTATION
     <IMS segment name 1>
     ....................
     <IMS segment name n>
```

C

IMS Database Definition Contents

1.1 Definition Subject

An *IMS database definition* (DBD) is a category of entry within the definition library serving as the focal point for information about IMS databases.

An *IMS database* is an ordered collection of IMS segments, arranged hierarchically to form discrete IMS database records. Each record can contain up to 15 levels in the segment hierarchy and up to 255 discrete IMS segment types. For a complete description of IMS facilities, including the databases, reference should be made to the IBM manuals.

1.2 Definition Contents

The contents of an IMS database definition include

- The primary names and aliases used to reference the IMS database
- General descriptive information identifying the criteria underlying the creation of the IMS database
- Symbolic references used to locate the IMS database definition within the definition library
- The names of project teams and organizational groups with an ongoing interest in the definition and its updates
- The names of organizational groups responsible for the ongoing accuracy and integrity of the definition
- References to the IMS segment types in the database and a definition of the segment hierarchy

```
           EXHIBIT: Contents of an IMS Database Definition
a)  External parameters
      <library entry identifier>
b)  Internal sections
    = = NAME: <IMS database name>
    = = ALIASES
          <alias name 1>(<context or usage comments>)
          ...........................................
          <alias name n>(<context or usage comments>)
    = = CLASSIFICATION
        IMS DATABASE DEFINITION
    = = DESCRIPTION
          <IMS database description>
    = = DEFINITION UPDATE SOURCE
          <source 1>(<date 1>)
          ....................
          <source n>(<date n>)
    = = USER ACCEPTANCE STATUS
          <status code 1>,<group 1>
          .........................
          <status code n>,<group n>
    = = DEFINITION RESPONSIBILITY
          <position title 1>
          .................
          <position title n>
    = =  STRUCTURE
            <IMS database name>
          XXXX  <IMS segment name 1-root segment>
          XXXX    <IMS segment name 2-indented>
          ....  ...........................
          XXXX    <IMS segment name n-indented>
    = = SOURCE SCHEMA
          <logical schema name 1>
          .......................
          <logical schema name n>
```

- References to other entries in the definition library associated in some specific manner with the IMS database

1.3   Definition Components

The following pages describe the fields and sections which make up an IMS database definition.

Library entry identifier. An 8-character alphanumeric identifier assigned to individual entries in the definition library.

This identifier takes the form XXXNNNNN, where XXX is a 3-character alphabetic field identifying the library volume containing the definition and NNNNN is a 5-character numeric field which serves as a unique identifier within a volume.

IMS database name. A composite field containing the names used to identify an IMS database.

The field takes the following form:

```
dddd(tttt)
```

dddd represents the formal name of the IMS database. It consists of from 1 to 50 characters constructed from the following character set:

- Uppercase alphabetic characters
- Numeric characters

tttt represents a descriptive name which can be used as an alternative to the formal name in user-oriented documentation. This name can be from 1 to 50 characters in length and is constructed from

- Uppercase alphabetic characters
- Numeric characters
- The special symbols hyphen, slash, and blank

Responsibility for assigning the IMS database name rests with the database administration section. In creating the names, the following conventions apply:

1. *Corporate Systems Standard K-10-10.* This standard requires the formal database name to be 4 characters in length and to be selected to reflect, in mnemonic form, the database subject. An example is the name EMPL given to the database containing employee information.

   This formal name is used as a subfield of both DBD and IMS segment names. DBD names take the form

   ```
   * Sdddd (primary database DBD NAME)
   * Sddddrr (index database DBD NAME)
   ```

   dddd is the 4-character formal name. S is a single-character prefix defined to represent the intended usage of the DBD. Values in the range A–Q are used for production DBD's. Values in the range R–Z are limited to "test" DBD's. rr is a 2-character postscript restricted to primary or secondary index databases. The value X1 identifies a primary index; the values X2–X9 are used for secondary indexes. The first 5 characters identify the related primary database.

   The IMS segment names take the form

   ```
   * ddddaaa
   ```

   dddd is the 4-character formal name. aaa is an arbitrary 3-character segment name which uniquely identifies the IMS physical database. The above naming convention applies to all IMS databases created by the DBA section.

2. *Local naming conventions.* Some databases implemented before June 1, 1979, the issue date for standard K-10-10, do not conform to the above conventions. For these databases, the formal *IMS database name* is defined as the DBD name.

3. *Naming conventions within commercial packages.* Databases included in systems purchased from external sources use naming conventions which are usually inconsistent with standard K-10-10. For these databases, the formal *IMS database name* is defined as the DBD name.

For all databases, the informal or descriptive name is derived from the primary database subject. For example, the database formally known as "POSN" is informally known as the "position database." By convention, this informal name is listed separately in the "aliases" section.

The specific representation of the IMS database name section is as follows:

```
= = NAME: <dictionary entry name>
= = <title of next section>
```

Aliases. A list of names used as alternate identifiers for the IMS database.

Each name consists of from 1 to 50 characters constructed from the following character set:

- Uppercase alphabetic characters.
- Numeric characters.
- The special symbols hyphen, comma, slash, period, and blank. The special symbols are used to format the name. For indexing and cross-referencing purposes, they are treated as blanks.

Names designated as aliases are terminated by any of the following:

- The last alphabetic or numeric character immediately preceding the leftmost bracket symbol (
- The last alphabetic or numeric character in positions 1 to 50 inclusive if the name contains no bracket symbol (

All characters to the right of and including the bracket symbol (are treated as blanks. Comments enclosed in brackets can be freely appended to an alias name but they cannot be embedded in the name.

Alias names provide a set of alternate identifiers for referencing IMS database definitions and IMS database representations. By appending comments to the names in the list, the primary usage of the alias name can be identified.

By convention the first name in the list should be the informal name for the IMS database. This ensures that the database is indexed by both its formal and its informal names.

The standard format for the section is as follows:

```
= = ALIASES
    <alias name 1>(<context or usage comments>)
    .........................................
    <alias name n>(<context or usage comments>)
= = <title of next section>
```

Library entry classification.   A descriptive code assigned to all library entries, identifying the type of definition.

For an IMS database definition, the classification code takes the value IMS DATABASE DEFINITION and is documented as follows:

```
= = CLASSIFICATION
    IMS DATABASE DEFINITION
= = <title of next section>
```

IMS database description.   A freeform narrative containing a description of the IMS database and its internal structure.

The description contains

1. A concise definition of the IMS database in a form suitable for use within a glossary. This definition occupies the first paragraph of the section and, ideally, should be 4 lines or less in length.
2. An overview of the IMS database segment structure identifying any major subgrouping of segments and the reasons for those groupings.
3. A description of the primary access paths within the IMS database, identifying

   - The primary or root key of the database and the database record sequencing relative to that key
   - The secondary index keys and the database record sequencing relative to those keys

4. Comments regarding the use of the IMS database.

IMS database descriptions are documented as follows:

```
= = DESCRIPTION
    <IMS database description line 1>
    ..............................
    <IMS database description line n>
= = <title of next section>
```

Definition update source. A composite structure identifying the individuals or groups who updated a library entry and the dates on which those updates were made.

A single occurrence of the structure is recorded for each update. It takes the form

```
<source>(<date>)
```

<source> is a 3-character field identifying the person or group who submitted the definition modification. Values of this field are conventionally derived from the initials of the person or group who first documented the definition or who subsequently submitted an update. The subfield <date> is a 6-digit date field in the format YYMMDD representing the date on which the definition was created or modified. By convention, values of this field normally reflect the date on which the changes were keyed into the definition library.

The specific representation of update information takes the form

```
= = DEFINITION UPDATE SOURCE
    <source 1>(<date 1>)
    ...................
    <source n>(<date n>)
= = <title of next section>
```

User acceptance status. A composite structure identifying the project teams or organizational groups who created the definition or who must be informed of its subsequent updates.

The structure is used

1. As the basis for propagating definition changes to support groups who may be affected by the proposed modifications.

2. To control the evolution of definition library entries from their initial form to the final versions accepted on a corporate basis

A single occurrence of the structure is recorded for each group. It takes the form

```
<status code>,<group name>
```

<status code> is a 1-character code representing the degree of acceptance of the library entry relative to the group identified by <group name>. It can take the following values:

Code	Meaning
I	The library entry represents a preliminary definition proposed by the associated systems development group. The definition may be changed at will by the team with no consultation with other users.
P	The library entry represents a working definition created or modified by the associated group. The definition may be changed, but only after consultation with all users indicating an acceptance code of P or A.
A	The library entry in its current form has been accepted as a working definition by the associated group. Changes in the definition can only be made after consultation with that group.
C	The library entry in its current form is ready for final review and acceptance by the group charged with responsibility for its ongoing integrity.
E	The library entry has been accepted by the groups assigned definition responsibility. Any further changes must be explicitly approved by those groups.

Status codes C and E are restricted to use in corporate library volumes. Status codes P and A can appear in any library volumes, while status code I is restricted to project library volumes.

User acceptance status information is assigned by data administration, on request and after consultation with the groups affected by a proposed status change. For definitions in a project library volume, if no status information exists, the definition is assumed to have status code I for the group to which the library volume belongs.

The specific representation of acceptance status information takes the form

```
= = USER ACCEPTANCE STATUS
      <status code 1>,<group 1>
      . . . . . . . . . . . . . . . . . . . . . .
      <status code n>,<group n>
= = <title of next section>
```

Definition responsibility. A set of references to the organizational groups charged with the responsibility for the accuracy and ongoing integrity of a definition.

References consist of a maximum of 50 characters derived from the position titles of the organizational groups. These position titles are obtained from the organization charts maintained by the personnel department.

Definition responsibility references are used to establish a relationship between a library entry and the organizational groups identified as the definitive source of information about the meaning and use of the IMS database. No changes can be made in a library entry after its acceptance by these groups, without their prior approval.

The standard representation for definition responsibility information is

```
= = DEFINITION RESPONSIBILITY
     <position title 1>
     ................
     <position title n>
= = <title of next section>
```

IMS database structure. A collection of IMS segment type names, arranged in hierarchical notation and identifying the segment types within an IMS database and its internal structure.

The section is documented as shown below.

1. *Basic notation.*

```
        <IMS database name>
   XXXX <IMS segment type name 1-root segment indented>
   XXXX <IMS segment type name n-root segment indented>
```

The IMS database name always occupies the first line of the section and serves as the anchor point for identing the subsequent IMS segment type names. Each level of indentation represents one level in the segment hierarchy. Dependencies between segments are reflected by relative differences in their indentation. For example, if B1, B2, and B3 in IMS database PQR are dependent upon A1 and if C1 is dependent upon B2, then database PQR is described as follows:

```
   PQR
   XXXX  A1
   XXXX    B1
   XXXX    B2
   XXXX      C1
   XXXX    B3
```

Note that B1, B2, and B3 are indented by the same amount relative to A1 and that C1 is indented with respect to B2. In addition, for consistency, A1 is indented 1 level with respect to PQR, signifying it is the highest level or root segment of the database.

Field XXXX denotes a relationship description value describing the association between a segment and its parent 1 level higher in the hierarchy. In the example, the value of XXXX for C1 describes its relationship to B2. The values of XXXX for B1, B2, and B3, in turn, describe the associations between those segments and segment A1. For IMS databases, XXXX can take the following values:

XXXX	Interpretation
OOAA	For each occurrence of the parent there must be one and only one occurrence of the dependent.
OOSA	For each occurrence of the parent there may be zero occurrences or a single occurrence of the dependent.
OMAA	For each occurrence of the parent there must be at least one occurrence of the dependent, and there may be many.
OMSA	For each occurrence of the parent there may be any number of occurrences of the dependent, including zero.

For the parent-dependent relationship B2–C1 in the example above, the values of XXXX for C1 are interpreted as follows:

XXXX	B1 occurrences	C1 occurrences
OOAA	1	1
OOSA	1	0,1
OMAA	1	$1,2\ldots n$
OMSA	1	$0,1\ldots n$

2. *Treatment of multilevel dependencies.* Dependencies between segments are represented by indentation. For direct relationships between two segments, single-level indentation is used. For example,

```
  . . . . X1       or    . . . .  Y1
 OMSA      Y1           OMSA      X1
 OOAA         Z1        OOAA         Z1
```

The first structure means that for an occurrence of X1 there can be many occurrences of Y1, and for each occurrence of Y1 there must always be an occurrence of Z1. The second structure has the roles of Y1 and X1 interchanged. The choice of form depends upon whether X1 or Y1 is viewed as the higher-level segment. The left form considers X1 the major key; the right form places Y1 in that role. Up to 15 levels of nesting can be used, but experience suggests that anything more than 4 levels in a physical database should be treated with caution.

3. *Treatment of comments.* General comments can be freely added to the structured description. They can take one of two forms:

```
  . . . . P1
 OOAA      Q1 (this is the first comment type)
 OMSA      R1
```

```
          This is the second type of comment
     OMSA   S1
```

The first form consists of bracketed text appended to an IMS segment type name. It is used to qualify the segment name or to provide additional descriptive information.

The second form consists of unbracketed text on a line with a blank relationship description field. This form can be used anywhere within the section, and blank lines are acceptable. It is used for footnotes or explanatory text or to improve the presentation of the database structure.

4. *Unresolved relationship descriptions.* Throughout the earlier sub-sections, specific values of the relationship description field XXXX have been introduced to serve various needs. If a suitable value cannot be assigned or if the value is irrelevant, two options are open.

The first option is to leave the field blank, i.e., to treat each segment name as a comment. Database structure can be expressed by indentation, but this method has the disadvantage that many of the mechanized cross-reference facilities, particularly error and warning diagnostics, will not be fully effective.

The second and recommended option is to set the field value to four hyphens, ----. This identifies the associated text as a group component name and supports the full cross-referenced and diagnostic facilities.

The standard representation of the section is as follows:

```
=  =  STRUCTURE
      <IMS database name>
      XXXX  <indented IMS segment type name 1>
      ...................................
      XXXX  <indented IMS segment type name n>
```

Note: The relationship description values used for IMS databases are a subset of the values which can be used to describe a relationship between any two objects.

Source schema. A list of names identifying the logical schemas of which the IMS database is a component.

The names in the list must correspond to the names associated with logical schema definitions stored elsewhere in the definition library.

The standard format for the section is as follows:

```
=  =  SOURCE SCHEMA
      <logical schema name 1>
      ........................
      <logical schema name n>
```

D

Logical Schema Definition Contents

1.1 Definition Subjects

A logical schema definition is a category of entry in the definition library describing a collection of logical groups which form the basis of a physical representation. This representation can be an IMS database or a logical file.

Each logical schema consists of one or more logical groups, usually arranged hierarchically. The groups included in the schema, and their interrelationships, are dictated by the entity model and the local data-access requirements built into the IMS database or other physical file.

1.2 Definition Contents

The components of logical schema definition include

- The primary name and aliases used to reference the logical schema
- General descriptive information identifying the criteria underlying the creation of the logical schema
- The names of project teams, users, and organizational groups with an ongoing interest in the definition and its updates
- The names of organizational groups responsible for the ongoing accuracy and integrity of the definition
- References to the logical groups in the schema and their internal relationships
- References to the IMS databases and logical files derived from the logical schema

```
            EXHIBIT: Contents of a Logical Schema Definition
a) External Parameters
        <library entry identifier>
b) Internal sections
   = = NAME: <logical schema name>
   = = ALIASES
        <alias name 1>(<context or usage comments>)
        ...........................................
        <alias name n>(<context or usage comments>)
   = = CLASSIFICATION
        LOGICAL SCHEMA DEFINITION
   = = DESCRIPTION
        <logical schema description>
   = = DEFINITION UPDATE SOURCE
        <source 1>(<date 1>)
        ..................
        <source n>(<date n>)
   = = USER ACCEPTANCE STATUS
        <status code 1>,<group 1>
        ......................
        <status code n>,<group n>
   = = DEFINITION RESPONSIBILITY
        <position title 1>
        ..................
        <position title n>
   = = CONTENTS
        <logical schema name>
        XXXX <indented logical group name 1>
        .....................................
        XXXX <indented logical group name n>
   = = IMS DATABASE REPRESENTATION
        <IMS database name 1>
        ..................
        <IMS database name n>
   = = LOGICAL FILE REPRESENTATION
        <logical file name 1>
        ..................
        <logical file name n>
```

1.3   Definition Components

The following pages describe the fields and sections which make up a
logical schema definition.

Library entry identifier. An 8-character alphanumeric identifier assigned to individual entries in the systems development reference
library.

This identifier takes the form XXXNNNNN, where XXX is a 3-character
alphabetic field identifying the library volume containing the definition and NNNNN is a 5-character numeric field which serves as a unique
identifier within a volume.

Logical schema name. A symbolic or descriptive name conventionally used to identify the logical schema.

A logical schema name consists of from 1 to 50 characters constructed from the following character set:

- Uppercase alphabetic characters
- Numeric characters
- The special symbols hyphen, slash, and blank. The special symbols are used to format the name. For indexing and cross-referencing purposes, they are treated as blanks.

A logical schema name is terminated by any of the following:

- The last alphabetic or numeric character immediately preceding the leftmost bracket symbol (
- The last alphabetic or numeric character in positions 1 to 50 inclusive if the name contains no bracket symbol (

All characters to the right of and including the bracket symbol (are treated as blanks. Comments and qualification, enclosed by the bracket symbol (and) can be freely appended to a logical schema name but cannot be embedded in the name.

All names longer than 50 characters must be truncated, or their length reduced to 50 characters or less using standard abbreviations. When abbreviations are used, the full name should be explicitly stated in the logical schema description.

Logical schema names must be selected within the guidelines below.

1. The name must be unique within the definition library.
2. The name must take the following form:
   AAAA   A descriptive name with no embedded commas. A typical example would be the name ICM EMPLOYEE SCHEMA.
3. The name should be concise but sufficiently descriptive that a user can gain a general appreciation of its contents and use without reference to the full definition.
4. Abbreviations within the name should be limited to situations in which the full name would exceed the maximum allowable length for a logical schema name.

The specific representation of the logical schema name section is as follows:

```
= = NAME: <dictionary entry name>
= = <title of next section>
```

Aliases. A list of names used as alternate identifiers for the logical schema.

Each name consists of from 1 to 50 characters constructed from the following character set:

- Uppercase alphabetic characters
- Numeric characters
- The special symbols hyphen, comma, slash, period, and blank. The special symbols are used to format the name. For indexing and cross-referencing purposes, they are treated as blanks.

Names designated as aliases are terminated by any of the following:

- The last alphabetic or numeric character immediately preceding the leftmost bracket symbol (
- The last alphabetic or numeric character in positions 1 to 50 inclusive if the name contains no bracket symbol (

All characters to the right of and including the bracket symbol (are treated as blanks. Comments enclosed in brackets can be freely appended to an alias name, but they cannot be embedded in the name.

Alias names provide a set of alternate identifiers for referencing logical schema definitions and logical schema representations. By appending comments to the names in the list, the primary usage of the alias name can be identified.

The standard format for the section is as follows:

```
= = ALIASES
    <alias name 1>(<context or usage comments>)
    ...........................................
    <alias name n>(<context or usage comments>)
= = <title of next section>
```

Logical schema description. A freeform narrative containing a description of the logical schema.

The description contains

1. A concise narrative of the objectives of the logical schema and how the logical schema will satisfy the user's requirements.
2. An overview of the entities and the entity relationships that make up the logical schema.
3. A statement of the criteria used in the formation of the logical schema. These are documented in order that future changes to the logical schema can be assessed relative to the initial criteria.

Logical schema descriptions are documented as follows

```
= = DESCRIPTION
    <logical schema description line 1>
    . . . . . . . . . . . . . . . . . . . . . . . . . . . . . . . . . .
    <logical schema description line n>
= = <title of next section>
```

Definition update source. A composite structure identifying the individuals or groups who updated a library entry and the dates on which those updates were made.

A single occurrence of the structure is recorded for each update. It takes the form

```
<source>(<date>)
```

<source> is a 3-character field identifying the person or group who submitted the definition modification. Values of this field are conventionally derived from the initials of the person or group who first documented the definition or who subsequently submitted an update. The subfield <date> is a 6-digit date field in the format YYMMDD, representing the date on which the definition was created or modified. By convention, values of this field normally reflect the date on which the changes were keyed into the definition library.

The specific representation of update information takes the form

```
= = DEFINITION UPDATE SOURCE
    <source 1>(<date 1>)
    . . . . . . . . . . . . . . . . . . . . . . .
    <source n>(<date n>)
= = <title of next section>
```

User Acceptance Status. A composite structure identifying the project teams or organizational groups who created the definition or who must be informed of its subsequent updates.

The structure is used

1. As the basis for propagating definition changes to support groups who may be affected by the proposed modifications
2. To control the evolution of definition library entries from their initial form to the final versions accepted on a corporate basis

A single occurrence of the structure is recorded for each group. It takes the form

```
<status code>,<group name>
```

<status code> is a 1-character code representing the degree of acceptance of the library entry relative to the group identified by <group name>. It can take the following values:

Code	Meaning
I	The library entry represents a preliminary definition proposed by the associated systems-development group. The definition may be changed at will by the team with no consultation with other users.
P	The library entry represents a working definition created or modified by the associated group. The definition may be changed, but only after consultation with all users indicating an acceptance code of P or A.
A	The library entry in its current form has been accepted as a working definition by the associated group. Changes in the definition can only be made after consultation with that group.
C	The library entry in its current form is ready for final review and acceptance by the group charged with responsibility for its ongoing integrity.
E	The library entry has been accepted by the groups assigned definition responsibility. Any further changes must be explicitly approved by those groups.

Status codes C and E are restricted to use in corporate library volumes. Status codes P and A can appear in all library volumes, while status code I is restricted to project library volumes.

User acceptance status information is assigned by data administration, on request and after consultation with the groups affected by a proposed status change. For definitions in a project library volume, if no status information exists, the definition is assumed to have status code I for the group to which the library volume belongs.

The specific representation of acceptance status information takes the form

```
= = USER ACCEPTANCE STATUS
    <status code 1>,<group 1>
    . . . . . . . . . . . . . . . . . . . . .
    <status code n>,<group n>
= = <title of next section>
```

Definition responsibility. A set of references to the organizational groups charged with the responsibility for the accuracy and ongoing integrity of a definition.

References consist of a maximum of 50 characters derived from the position titles of the organizational groups. These position titles are obtained from the organizational charts maintained by the personnel department.

Definition responsibility references are used to establish a relationship between a library entry and the organizational groups identified as the definitive source of information about the logical schema's meaning and use. No changes can be made in a library entry after its acceptance by these groups, without their prior approval.

The standard representation for definition responsibility information is

```
= = DEFINITION RESPONSIBILITY
    <position title 1>
    ..................
    <position title n>
= = <title of next section>
```

Logical schema contents. A collection of logical groups, arranged in hierarchial notation, identifying the components of the logical schema and their internal relationships.

The section is documented as shown below.

1. *Basic notation.*

```
<logical schema name>
XXXX <component name 1, indented to appropriate level>
XXXX <component name n, indented to appropriate level>
```

The logical schema name always occupies the first line of the section and serves as the anchor point for indenting subsequent component names. Each level of indentation represents 1 level in the component hierarchy. Dependencies between components are reflected by relative differences in their indentation. For example, if B1, B2, and B3 in logical schema PQRSAAA are dependent upon A1 and if C1 is dependent upon B2, then group type PQRSAAA is described as follows:

```
        PQRSAAA
XXXX    A1
XXXX      B1
XXXX      B2
XXXX        C1
XXXX      B3
```

Note that B1, B2, and B3 are indented by the same amount relative to A1 and that C1 is indented with respect to B2. In addition, for consistency, A1 is indented 1 level with respect to PQRSAAA, signifying that it is the highest-level component of the schema.

Field XXXX denotes a relationship description value describing the association between a schema component and its parent 1 level higher in the hierarchy. In the example, the value of XXXX for C1 describes its relationship to B2. The values of XXXX for B1, B2, and B3, in turn, describe the associations between those components and component A1.

For logical schemas, XXXX can take the following values:

XXXX	Interpretation
OOAA	For each occurrence of the parent there must be one and only one occurrence of the dependent.
OOSA	For each occurrence of the parent there may be zero occurrences or a single occurrence of the dependent.
OMAA	For each occurrence of the parent there must be at least one occurrence of the dependent and there may be many.
OMSA	For each occurrence of the parent there may be any number of occurrences of the dependent, including zero.

For the parent-dependent relationship B2–C1 in the example above, the values of XXXX for C1 are interpreted as follows:

XXXX	B1 occurrences	C1 occurrences
OOAA	1	1
OOSA	1	0,1
OMAA	1	$1,2\ldots n$
OMSA	1	$0,1\ldots n$

2. *Treatment of multilevel dependencies.* Dependencies between schema components are represented by indentation. For direct relationships between two components, single-level indentation is used. For example,

```
    .  .  .  . G1
OMSA        H1
```

The example indicates that occurrences of H1 are dependent upon occurrences of G1.

For dependencies involving three or more components, multilevel indentation must be used. If Z1 depends on both Y1 and X1, then the dependency can be expressed in two forms:

```
    .  .  .  . X1        or     .  .  .  . Y1
OMSA        Y1                OMSA        X1
OOAA        Z1                OOAA        Z1
```

The first structure means that for an occurrence of X1 there can be many occurrences of Y1 and for each occurrence of Y1 there must always be an occurrence of Z1. The second structure has the roles of Y1 and X1 interchanged. the choice of form depends upon whether X1 or Y1 is viewed as the major key. The left form considers XI the major key; the right form places Y1 in that role.

This nesting of levels can proceed to any depth, although experience suggests that anything more than 4 levels should be treated with caution.

3. *Treatment of subgroups.* It is a common requirement to identify and treat a subgrouping of components as a higher-level component in its own right. This subgrouping is documented as follows:

```
 .  .  .  .  A1
OMAA        (subgroup XYZ)
OOAA           B1
OOAA           D1
OMSA        E1
```

(subgroup XYZ) identifies a subgroup which contains one occurrence of B1 and one of D1. The subgroup as a whole is defined to be a dependent of A1, and the relationship specification OMAA indicates there must always be at least one occurrence of that subgroup for each occurrence of A1. Each component of the subgroup must be indented at least 1 level with respect to the subgroup name, and deeper nesting may exist if the subgroup itself contains internal dependencies. The first group component at the same level as or a higher level than the subgroup name terminates the subgroup and is not considered a subgroup component. In the example, subgroup XYZ is terminated by E1, but although E1 is a dependent of A1, it is not a component of XYZ.

In effect, subgroups can be considered single components at all higher levels. They are particularly useful for documenting repeating groups or sets of group components which are considered indivisible.

4. *Mutually exclusive group components.* Occasionally, a logical schema references mutually exclusive components. Either one component must be present or the other, but not both. This is expressed as follows:

```
 .  .  .  .  A1
OOAA        B1
 -OR-          C1
```

A1 has dependents B1 and C1 which are mutually exclusive. For each occurrence of A1 there must be an occurrence of B1 or an occurrence of C1 but not both. This association between B1 and C1 is represented by the −OR− symbol which takes the place of the usual relationship description. The OOAA associated with B1 applies to the total set of components linked by the −OR− symbol. More complicated structures can be produced by linking together subgroups and individual group components. As an example,

```
.  .  .  .    A1
OOAA          B1
−OR−          (subgroup PQR)
OOAA          P1
−OR−            Q1
−OR−          (subgroup XYZ)
OMSA          X1
```

An occurrence of A1 has as its dependents one and only one occurrence of either B1, subgroup PQR, or subgroup XYZ. PQR consists of an occurrence of P1 or an occurrence of Q1. XYZ consists of many occurrences of X1.

5. *Treatment of comments.*   General comments can be freely added to the schema. They can take one or two forms:

```
.  .  .  .    P1
OOAA          A1(this is the first comment type)
OMSA          R1
              This is the second type of comment
OMSA          S1
```

The first form consists of bracketed text appended to a logical schema component name. It is used to qualify the component name or to provide additional descriptive information.

The second form consists of unbracketed text on a line with a blank relationship description field. This form can be used anywhere within the section, and blank lines are acceptable. It is used for footnotes or explanatory text, or to improve the presentation of the segment structure.

6. *Unresolved relationship descriptions.*   Throughout the earlier subsections, specific values of the relationship description field XXXX have been introduced to serve various needs. If a suitable value cannot be assigned or if the value is irrelevant, two options are open.

The first option is to leave the field blank, i.e., to treat each component name as a comment. Group structure can be expressed by indentation, but this method has the disadvantage that many of the mechanized cross-reference facilities, particularly error and warning diagnostics, will not be fully effective.

The second and recommended option is to set the field value to four hyphens, –––. This identifies the associated text as a schema component name and supports the full cross-reference and diagnostic facilities.

The standard representation of the section is as follows:

```
= = CONTENTS
    <logical schema name>
    XXXX <indented logical group name 1>
    ...................................
    XXXX <indented logical group name n>
= = <title of next section>
```

IMS database representation. A list of names identifying the IMS databases derived from the logical schema. The names adhere to the convention outlined in the IMS database definition for naming databases.

The standard representation of the section is as follows:

```
= = IMS DATABASE PRESENTATION
    <IMS database name 1>
    ....................
    <IMS database name n>
= = <title of next section>
```

Logical file representation. A list of names identifying the logical files derived from the logical schema. The names adhere to the convention outlined in the logical file definition for naming logical files.

The standard format for the section is as follows:

```
= LOGICAL FILE REPRESENTATION
  <logical file name 1>
  ....................
  <logical file name n>
```

BIBLIOGRAPHY

Atre, S.: *Data Base: Structured Techniques for Design, Performance, and Management*, John Wiley, New York, 1980.

Braithwaite, K. S.: *Data Administration*, John Wiley, New York, 1985.

————: *An implementation of a Data Dictionary to Support Databases Designed Using the Entity-Relationship (E-R) Approach*, North-Holland Publishers, New York, 1983.

————: "Resolution of Conflicts in Data Ownership and Sharing in a Corporate Environment," AGT Technical Memo, 1983.

Canning, R. G.: "A New View of Data Dictionaries," *EDP Analyzer*, July 1981.

Champine, G. A.: *Distributed Computer Systems*, North-Holland Publishers, New York, 1980.

Datacom/DD: *Data Dictionary and Directory System Concepts and Facilities*, Applied Data Research, Inc., Dallas, Texas, 1978.

Datamanager: *Users Manual*, MSP, Inc., Lexington, Mass., 1981.

DB/DC: *Data Dictionary—General Information Manual*, IBM Corp., San Jose, Calif., 1978.

Durell, W.: *Data Administration*, McGraw-Hill, New York, 1985.

ICL: *Data Dictionary System Reference Manual*, International Computers Ltd., London, 1978.

Intel: *Integrated Data Dictionary Overview*, Intel Systems Corp., Austin, Texas, 1980.

Leong-Hong, B.: *Data Dictionary/Directory Systems*, John Wiley, New York, 1982.

Madnick, S. E.: *Computer Security*, Academic Press, New York, 1979.

Miller, M.: "A Survey of Distributed Data Base Management," Information and Management, 1978.

Morgan, H.: "The Interconnected Future: Data Processing, Office Automation, Personal," Wharton School, Pennsylvania, Working Paper 78-07-04, 1978.

Ross, R.: *Data Dictionary Systems and Data Administration*, Amacom, New York, 1981.

Sibley, E. H.: "Data Element Dictionaries for Information Interface," *Information Processing*, January 1974.

UCC-10: *User's Guide*, University Computing Co., Austin, Texas, 1977.

Wertz, C. J.: *The Data Dictionary—Concepts and Uses*, QED Information Sciences, Inc., Massachusetts, 1986.

Index

About the Author

Ken Braithwaite is a professor of computer science at the University of Alberta, Canada. Presently, he is on leave at Software Design Associates in Union, New Jersey. Dr. Braithwaite has over 19 years' experience in data processing. Since 1974 he has specialized in data administration and management of data as a resource.